MAKING
PEACE
WITH THE IMAGE
IN THE MIRROR

MAKING PEACE

WITH THE IMAGE
IN THE MIRROR

SPIRITUAL SOLUTIONS FOR SELF-ESTEEM AND INNER ACCEPTANCE

Steven R. Hawks

BOOKCRAFT

Although the students named in this book are fictitious characters, they symbolize the thoughts, feelings, and struggles of many real students who have participated in the author's weight-loss classes over the past ten years.

Library of Congress Cataloging-in-Publication Data

Hawks, Steven R.
   Making peace with the image in the mirror / Steven R. Hawks.
      p.   cm.
Includes bibliographical references and index.
   ISBN 1-57345-941-0 (pbk.)
1. Body image.   2. Body image in women.   3. Church of Jesus Christ of Latter-day Saints—Doctrines.   4. Mormon Church—Doctrines.   I. Title.
BF697.5.B63 H38 2001
306.4—dc21

2001002392

Printed in the United States of America   54459-6797
10 9 8 7 6 5 4 3 2 1

For my wife, Jaylyn

CONTENTS

INTRODUCTION

Mirror, mirror, on the wall,
Who in this realm is the fairest of all?
—Snow White's stepmother

Ever since I was a boy I have been deeply attached to fairy tales. Some of my favorite childhood memories include going to the drive-in movies with my family in our old Rambler station wagon and watching the great Disney animated classics—*Bambi, Snow White, Sleeping Beauty.* As my own children came along, I wanted to share with them the same happiness that these stories and experiences had brought me. Toward that end, I purchased several fairy tale books and read them often to my young children.

Over the years I have come to appreciate the allegorical nature of these tales and the deeply meaningful insights that they possess, insights that in some cases are perhaps more relevant to us than to the peasants who first heard them. For example, as I read to my little girl Jessica the story of Snow White from *The Complete Fairy Tales of the Brothers Grimm,*[1] I was compelled to reflect upon the deeper meaning of the story.

Once upon a time, the fairy tale begins, there was a girl named Snow White. Sadly, the girl's mother died soon after she was born. A year later, the king married another woman and made her the new queen and, by default, Snow White's stepmother. This new queen was in possession of a magic mirror that could tell her how beautiful she was. "You, my queen, are the fairest of all," it would say whenever she asked.

But then one day, the mirror told the queen that someone else was "a thousand times more fair" than she was. At this point in the story, the Brothers Grimm note, "the queen shuddered and became yellow and green with envy. From that hour on, her hate was so great that her heart throbbed and turned in her breast. Like weeds, the envy and arrogance grew so dense in her heart that she no longer had any peace, day or night."

"That's terrible," Jessica said quietly after hearing this passage. I agreed that the new queen had definitely taken a major turn for the worse. But interestingly there is not one word about the new queen being evil or corrupt or wicked before this fateful interaction with the mirror. It was her incessant need for approval from the mirror that encouraged her subsequent wickedness. Once she felt that her appearance was no longer adequate, she lost her morals, her affection for others, and her decency as her life spiraled downward in never-ending attempts to regain approval from the looking glass.

In the end, the queen was forced to witness Snow White's happy marriage, and then she was executed. According to the final lines of the story, "the queen was so petrified with fright that she could not budge. Iron slippers had already been heated over a fire, and they were brought over to her with tongs. Finally, she had to put on the red-hot slippers and dance until she fell down dead."

My little Jessica thought this was pretty stiff punishment, but it was the queen's obsession with the mirror that caused her terrible destruction. And that's where the analogy becomes relevant to us. Many of us are preoccupied with trying to obtain approval from the mirror. We are at war with the looking glass, and the battle may not end any better for us than it did for the wicked queen.

In a recent USA Today article, a TV personality complained that "when I looked at myself in the mirror, I was not thrilled with what I saw." (It seems that the wicked queen is not the only one with an interactive mirror.) "So I went ahead and got some plastic surgery," the celebrity continues, "like every other good person in America."[2]

And so the fixation begins. Our concern with trying to please the mirror has escalated to the point that all "good people" are expected to subject themselves to any procedure that might possibly increase contentment with their reflected image. The TV personality quoted above, for example, being dissatisfied with the results of plastic surgery now injects herself daily with harmful doses of human growth hormone (HGH). In addition, she takes "ten pills: six supplements and four prescription drugs." When the current regimen fails (as it ultimately will), new devices and potions will no doubt be sought.

It is all very reminiscent of the wicked queen who could not rest unless the magic mirror proclaimed her to be the most beautiful one of all. If one strategy failed, she tried a new one. She set aside morality, values, and personal integrity as each failure with the mirror led to the adoption of even more extreme tactics. "Like weeds, the envy and arrogance grew so dense in her heart that she no longer had any peace, day or night."

The USA Today article goes on for several pages to discuss the current schemes being used by those who are not "thrilled" with what they see in the mirror. Their attempts to look younger and otherwise positively influence the judgments of the looking glass include yoga; longevity diets; cranial massage; medicinal spas; laser treatments; a variety of implants, injections, and surgeries; and the application of "cosmeceuticals" (cosmetics with a variety of special longevity agents added). Will all the technology and money at our command make our chances of winning the battle with the mirror any greater than the wicked queen's? Or is it more likely that the culmination of our exertions will be analogous to "wearing red-hot slippers and dancing until we fall down dead"?

According to the Brothers Grimm, the wicked queen "no longer had any peace, day or night" due to her fear of not being the "fairest in the land." With uncanny similarity, Sarah Goldberg, a "typical" eighteen-year-old high school student, was quoted in *People Weekly* magazine as saying, "There's not a second in my life that I don't think about some aspect of how I look."[3] The words of the fairy tale and the words of the modern young woman are slightly different, but the sentiment is the same—both portray a desperate struggle for mastery over the mirror. In our society, the struggle is growing both in scale and in intensity, and the stakes are higher than ever.

There are many things that make us feel inadequate and unworthy—a threatening mirror among the rest. But if we allow such demons to compel and control us, we may exchange the positive opportunities afforded by this life for a destructive dance that drains us of vital energy and ultimately destroys us.

It is my hope (and sweet Jessica's) that we will not be caught in the same web that enmeshed Snow White's stepmother. It is important for us to heed the lesson that is taught by her downfall. The contest with the mirror is not the most worthy cause to which we can devote our strength. In order to free our attention for the truly important battles, it is time to make peace with the image in the mirror.

WAGING WAR WITH
THE MIRROR

Our dissatisfaction with the image in the mirror stems from several misconceptions. First, we feel that an imperfect image represents a genuine flaw in our nature that demands attention. Second, we believe that the supposed flaw requires attention because it has a direct bearing on our actual worth. Third, we assume that if we devote enough resources to the remediation of the flaw that it can be cured, or at least hidden adequately. Fourth, we believe that if the flaw is removed or hidden, the result will be a more valuable and worthwhile person. Finally, we think that if we increase our worth by eliminating our visible flaws, happiness and satisfaction with life will also be enhanced.

Section one of the book attempts to work through these misconceptions, and to clarify the true nature of the war with the mirror and explain why it is futile. It discusses the inner needs that we attempt to meet by enhancing personal attractiveness and defines the relationship between these needs and appearance.

CHAPTER ONE

A FAULTY BATTLE PLAN

'Tis easy to frame a good bold resolution;
But hard is the Task that concerns execution.
—Poor Richard's Almanac, 1742

I was in third grade the first time someone called me "fatty." I remember how much it hurt my feelings. It was the first time in my life that I felt my inherent nature was somehow flawed. But it wasn't the last time. Later, in eighth grade, my coach would yell at me during basketball practice: "Hey, Hawks, what are you doing wearing an inner tube around your belly, boy?" I would cringe with embarrassment at the laughs of my teammates. More recently, as a health professor at North Carolina State University, I was asked to teach classes on nutrition, activity, and weight control. How do you teach about those things with any credibility when you are fat? All this goes without mentioning my freckles, skinny legs, and shyness.

I could cite many other experiences and flaws, but the point is that feeling inadequate can seem like having a millstone around your neck. It's difficult to forget, and it makes it very hard to look up and see a blue sky. Everything that's worth having seems to be reserved for those with slender hips and clear complexions. Frequent consultations with the mirror provide consistent proof that I am not qualified. Ah, the mirror. If it were not for the mirror, I would not be able to discern my comparative inadequacy. Lacking a more substantial foe to conquer, I take up arms against the looking glass. If I can throw off its tyranny, perhaps I can find relief for my pain.

As with many others, my life has been an unrealized attempt to win the war with the mirror, living each day under a cloud of discouragement caused by being large, unattractive, or incapable, hoping someday that I will magically wake up to the reflection of a good-looking, competent person. Then I could casually step across the line and take my place among the beautiful people and bask in the warmth of love and happiness. Many have made serious plans to deprive the mirror of its merciless power, but with eyes down and head bowed, most fall short.

BUT HOW TO WAGE THE WAR?

Join me on a pivotal day at North Carolina State University (NCSU) in Raleigh, North Carolina, as I make plans to shatter the mirror into shards of impotency. It is ten years ago. Imagine two large men slowly jogging around the university track on a very hot, humid day. *Large* in this case is a polite understatement, and the term *jogging* is also used quite loosely. The fatal Southern humidity draws perspiration from them by the bucketful. I am the one laboring on the inside lane, a coveted position due to the slightly shorter distance required to complete each lap. My partner and fellow sufferer, Steve, struggles to keep up in the outside lane. We are easily recognized by the tightness of our gym shorts, which ultimately creep down until our fellow joggers yell at us, "Pull your shorts up." It is our first day of running, and we are surprised at how often the other runners pass us doing laps.

After several aborted attempts, Steve is finally able to gasp, one labored word at a time, "Why—in—the—world—are—we—doing—this?"

As an assistant professor of health education at NCSU, I am annoyed that such an obvious point would require elaboration. I try to time the words of my response so that they coincide with the availability of breath, "Because—we—are—too—fat."

As a biologist, Steve seldom accepts my health theories without a challenge. Red-faced, on the verge of heatstroke, he asks, "How do you know we are too fat?" A hundred yards later he concludes, "Even if we are too fat, there must be some other way to lose it."

By this time, having completed all of two laps, we determine that the activity of jogging must be taken up gradually, and we thereupon excuse ourselves to the locker room. Along the way I explain to my friend the supposed dangers of obesity and propose that we subject ourselves to two common measures of that disorder, namely the height-weight chart and the skin-fold calipers. A consultation with the Metropolitan Height-Weight Chart establishes the ideal weight for Steve at 160 pounds, while allowing me only 155. A further consultation with a balance scale shows that we both weigh in at about 200 pounds—well above the clinical measure for obesity (20 percent over ideal weight).

"Of course, the fallacy of height-weight charts," explains Steve, "is that they fail to take into account the individual who has extra amounts of lean body mass. In other words, most of what you see before you is solid muscle."

I then produce from my locker a newly calibrated device known as a skin-fold caliper. "Perhaps you would care to find out the truth of the matter?" I offer. Without showing much appetite for it, he at last complies. I had not had a great deal of experience with the instrument and soon ran into obstacles. The first measure was to be taken from the midsection of the abdomen, next to the navel. This particular piece of anatomy, especially among the obese, I discovered, does not conveniently lend itself to being pinched and calibrated. As Steve begins to giggle in response to my tentative measuring, the difficulty of the task grows proportionately. My request for silence is rewarded with a burst of belly laughter that shakes the dangling tool to the floor. A final attempt, Steve pinching with two hands and I with one, finally forces the distressed wedge of flesh in between the fully extended prongs of the caliper. My announcement to the gathering crowd that "we have seldom obtained such a reading on a human subject" is treated to a warm round of applause.

Subsequent measurements taken from the chest, legs, and arms prove no less dramatic. We were bruised and torn by the end of it, but at the same time sensible of the popularity we had achieved among the locker room crowd. Based on our best calculations, we were somewhere between 25 and 35 percent body fat, well above the ideal range for males of 12 to 14 percent. Any way you measured it, we were fat. In fact, we were clinically obese. I perhaps felt the shame of it a little more than Steve because I was a fat *health* professor; he was only a fat scientist. I was supposed to know better. Ever since third grade I had known I was overweight (the taunts of my classmates made that clear enough), but qualifying for the clinical designation of obesity at this time in my life was still painful.

We performed a final test that would provide ultimate proof of our obesity. "It is called the 'mirror test,'" I explained to Steve. "You stand before the mirror and jump up and down a couple of times. The magnitude of jiggling adiposity will serve as the test result." I will not insult the modesty of the reader with the details of this final degradation; suffice it to say that our efforts were successful both in dispersing the groaning spectators and in establishing ourselves as very fat and jiggly. The mirror was the final judge, and she had proclaimed her verdict—we were far from being the fairest in the land. My private war with the formidable looking glass escalated a few notches. The ever-present millstone was as heavy as ever.

I was preparing to apply for a position as a health professor at Utah State University, and I knew that showing up to the interview in a state of obesity would not improve my chances of being hired. It was time to do something. I was a health scientist at a major research university. Surely I could figure out the secret of this beast and throw off the yoke of obesity once and for all. I, too, could be slender. I would teach the mirror to sing praise, instead of mockery. The wicked queen had failed where I would be victorious. The way to wage war with the mirror is to lose weight, and I was ready for battle.

A FAULTY BATTLE PLAN

According to one popular survey, satisfaction with our image really is mostly about body size—as measured by how much we weigh. Ninety percent of happiness with our overall appearance is a direct function of the reading on the bathroom scale.[1] We seem to believe that if we can just lose weight, everything else will fall into place. But how did we come to care so deeply about how much we weigh? How did we end up at war with the looking glass, unable to fully enjoy life due to a deep dissatisfaction with our appearance? How did we get left outside the circle of happiness, with no apparent way to get in, just because of how much we weigh?

Why do we make it a daily ritual to place ourselves on a scale, like a prize turkey at the poultry shop? From what deep spring does the despair well up within us at the sight of the number that invariably seems to grow larger in spite of our most desperate attempts to make it grow smaller? How did that number gain the power to determine so completely our worth as human beings, the quality of our relationships, and our chances for happiness in this life?

Why do we at last turn away, our shoulders stooped in defeat, pacing restlessly like the evil queen in front of the mirror, knowing full well that the really nice clothes will never fit us and that the chances for altering the cruel truth of the scale in our favor are slim to none at all? Why does so much depend on our appearance as reflected in the mirror?

As a health professor (albeit a fat one) at North Carolina State University, I thought I knew the answer to these questions. It was just like I explained to Steve: how much we weigh can directly determine the quality of our physical health. It is a simple health issue, I thought. If we are overfat, and therefore conspicuously un-health conscious, it is to be expected that our common struggle, if not our moral imperative, should be to lose weight. We are justly condemned or honorably redeemed by the flashing red number that declares our poundage in the beacon of our digital scales.

And so Steve and I gave in to the pressure and bowed down to the idol of physical health. On bended knee we dedicated our lives to the noble quest for thinness. It was not a pleasant process, but six months later, based on a carefully regulated program of restricted calories and increased exercise, we had both dropped forty pounds. We had qualified for entrance into the golden circle of love. We didn't have to stand on the edge anymore. We had won the gold!

At least we thought we had won it, but nothing changed. Speaking for myself, I still wasn't happy with the image that greeted me from the looking glass. Love and happiness did not magically accompany the weight loss. A battle plan that simply focused on changing body size did not lead to victory. The mirror still had control, but I couldn't understand why. What else could I do?

DEFINING THE REAL FOE

First of all, we got some things wrong. The real foe in the war with the looking glass is not body size or even appearance. It turns out that there is more to lose than just physical bulk. The real foe is our underlying sense of inadequacy. Far more than our body weight, this is the burden that pins us down and keeps us from engaging in the most important battles. I found this out after starting my new position at Utah State University.

As a svelte new member of the USU health faculty, I was excited to learn that there were numerous opportunities to teach one-credit workshops on weekends. Having recently unlocked the secrets of weight loss and physical health, I was eager to share the message with the masses through this convenient new avenue.

As an ice breaker, and knowing full well that the answer was "health," I stood before the students who had registered for my first weight-control workshop and asked the question, "So why do you want to lose weight, anyway?"

After some hems and haws most students indicated that they just needed one extra credit and a weight-loss class seemed like an easy "A." "It doesn't really have much to do with actually wanting to lose weight," one student explained.

At the same time I made a mental note that either there were a heck of a lot more women than men who needed one extra credit (there was only one man in the class of 25) or else there was more to their involvement in my class than they were divulging. And so in a second attempt to get a meaningful discussion going, I asked them to write down the top three reasons that *other* people wanted to lose weight. (It is apparently easier to consider the weight-loss motives of others, as personal motives are too pure to be made a topic of common discussion.)

After lengthy consideration, we came up with a list of why *others* wanted to lose weight. It looked something like this:

• self-esteem	• pressure from boyfriend	• look good
• gain control	• feel good about yourself	• get dates
• get a good job	• pressure from spouse	

Because I was a health professor teaching a class listed under the health section in the course schedule, I was more than a little surprised to find that health had not even been mentioned as a reason to lose weight. At first I assumed that it was overlooked simply because it was so obvious. So I politely asked, "What about health?"

After a long pause an attractive young coed named Brittany patiently explained, "There may be someone out there somewhere who is genuinely concerned about losing weight for the sake of health, but that's not why we're here." She emphasized her observation with a toss of her head that made her long, brown hair fly over her shoulder.

As the faces of the other women lit up with smiles, I realized that either I had an atypical group of individuals in my class or my assumptions about weight-loss motivations needed some adjustment. To buy time, we played a *Sesame Street*–type game with the items on our chalkboard list: "Some of these things go together, some of these things are kind of the same."

By the time we were done, only three reasons for losing weight were listed on the board, and health still wasn't one of them. To my surprise, the three reasons, in rank-order, were

1. Appearance
2. Love and acceptance
3. Self-esteem

As first developed, my weight-control workshop dealt exclusively with activity levels, diet composition, and the relationship between obesity and physical health. This, after all, was the primary reason that I assumed everyone was concerned about body size. While the workshops were well received, it became increasingly obvious that motivations to control body size were not related to health. For my students weight loss was seen instead as a means toward other ends, specifically appearance, love and acceptance, and self-esteem. It became obvious that body size is not the true enemy. It is the sense of underlying inadequacy, for which body size and appearance become convenient scapegoats. Our appearance is a straw man that we grapple with so that we don't have to confront our underlying feelings of inadequacy.

As I reflected on my own weight-loss efforts in light of this discussion, I had to admit that, even more than health, my motivation had perhaps been the desire to look good and feel better about myself. Even though I did lose weight, my appearance was still flawed, at least in my own estimation, and my self-esteem was as low as ever. Would weight loss among my students lead to the realization of their expectations? Or would they still be locked in combat with the looking glass, as I was?

THE RISING TIDE OF INADEQUACY

Even though our appearance is not the real foe that deprives us of love and contentment, there are some very strong social forces that drive us to conclude that physical attractiveness is a prerequisite for happiness. Out of curiosity, and with respect for the real concerns of my students, I began to read the literature on body image and self-esteem. I was surprised and saddened to come across a variety of popular and scientific surveys that all came to similar conclusions—namely, women experience very powerful feelings of inadequacy as a result of how they look:[2]

• The number one wish of teenage girls is to lose weight and keep it off.

• 80 percent of ten-year-old girls diet.

• The number one concern of adult women is body size.

• The majority of women are very dissatisfied with their appearance.

• 80 percent of American women diet and 50 percent are on a diet at any given time.

• The self-esteem of women plummets in adolescence due to body dissatisfaction.

• 8 million Americans suffer from anorexia or bulimia.

• 75 percent of women with normal weight feel that they need to lose more weight.

The following is according to Mary Pipher, best-selling author of the book *Reviving Ophelia,* which examines the psychological and physical health of teenage girls, "Research shows that virtually all women are ashamed of their bodies. It used to be adult women, teenage girls, who were ashamed, but now you see the shame down to very young girls—10, 11 years old."[3]

As I look out over the students who come to my weight-control class, many of whom are very attractive even by today's strict standards, I am impressed by the consistent observation that no matter how beautiful they look, no matter how "healthy" their body size is, very few feel that they are okay or that they are thin enough. They come to my class and say, "Please show me a way to lose more weight." Just as it did to the wicked queen in Snow White, the mirror continually whispers the message to these students that they do not look good enough.

I realized that it was not the health profession that was setting body weight standards. Instead, it was the fashion industry and everyone else who supports the narrow image of beauty it portrays. We have all come to believe, at least a little, in the rewards that our society promises if we prevail in our struggles with the mirror.

But whether the concern is improving physical health or conforming to social pressure, the consequences of being overweight seem significant, if not devastating. And so, not really knowing what else to do, I faithfully carried on—preaching the gospel of weight control from a health promotion perspective to a choir of students who were mostly interested in trying to obtain the social rewards of sculpting an ideal body. This was not good.

Conclusion

And thus it all began with that pivotal day in the hot sun of Raleigh, North Carolina, followed by new insights from my early courses in weight management at Utah State University. For more than ten years, I have been trying to understand the determinants of self-worth and the relationship between feeling unattractive and being unhappy. The investigation has resulted in many insights. Some deal with the biological nature of obesity, including its causes and its relationship to health, but many more deal with the spiritual nature of love and acceptance, self-worth, the realization of spiritual poten-tial, and how all these things are influenced by our relationship with the mirror.

Deep down inside I guess I always knew that there was more to it than just physical health. I knew it from personal, ongoing concern with body size and appearance that began way back in third grade. It is my hope that by setting down an account of my own flawed and yet unfinished battle with the mirror, other warriors will be able to plan their strategies wisely, avoid pitfalls and crooked trails, over-come the many fallacies that obscure the way, and at last make peace with their own reflection.

SUMMARY

Feeling inadequate or unattractive represents a serious challenge to self-esteem. It feels like a millstone around our necks, forever pulling our gaze downward. We feel excluded and unworthy of love. The obvious solution to our dilemma is to change how we look, with the mirror acting as the final judge of our success. Like the wicked queen in Snow White, we become increasingly obsessed with the feedback the mirror provides until it ultimately becomes the organizing principle around which our lives revolve. We declare war on the image in the mirror and fight a running battle, but we never win.

Sometimes we manufacture "pure" motivations for trying to change our appearance, such as "We are trying to be more healthy." But the truth is that "health" (and other justifications we might fabricate) are mere smoke screens that mask our real desire to look good so that we can meet our needs for love, acceptance, and self-esteem.

CHAPTER TWO

THE EVIL CHAIN OF ASSUMPTIONS

---

*If we start right, it is very easy to go right all the time; but if we start
wrong we may go wrong, and it be a hard matter to get right.*
—Joseph Smith

It hurts deeply to feel like you have been pushed outside the
circle of love because your appearance makes you unworthy of inclu-
sion. Many of us feel like we have been pushed out, and many more
join us each day. The circle of love and acceptance gets ever smaller,
while the number of those on the periphery just keeps growing.
Perhaps it is because the fashion industry and the media generally
portray only one acceptable body type: thin—usually tall and thin.

BODY DISSATISFACTION IN THE UNITED STATES

While the average woman in the United States is 5 feet 4 inches
tall and weighs 142 pounds, the average model is 5 feet 9 inches tall
and weighs 110 pounds.[1] And if anything, the discrepancy between
"average" and the "media ideal" is growing larger over time. For
example, the average body mass index of Miss America contestants
has gone from the healthy range of 20 to 25 from the 1920s to the
1950s, down to the medically undernourished range of 16 to 19 in
more recent decades.[2] It's estimated that less than five percent of the
population has a natural body size that will qualify them for admission

into the circle of acceptability portrayed by the media. It is small wonder that more and more people feel like they are getting left out.

Hollywood director Joel Schumacher says, "Sophia Loren and Marilyn Monroe could not get a job today. Their agents would tell them, 'Go on a diet, get a trainer.'" This constant push for an ultra thin body is wearing down the self-esteem of today's women. It is not surprising then, that even though he has worked with Demi Moore, Julia Roberts, and Sandra Bullock, Schumacher says, "I have never worked with a young woman who thought she was (a) beautiful, or (b) thin enough."[3]

Size Discrimination

The pressure for women to be thin goes beyond the desire to look like beauty queens or Hollywood stars. It is a matter of survival. A seven-year study published in the *New England Journal of Medicine* found that overweight women complete less schooling, are 20 percent less likely to get married, have 10 percent higher rates of household poverty, and earn almost $7,000 less than their slimmer counterparts.[4]

Even in an age characterized by great concern for human rights and political correctness, it seems apparent that the obese and socially unattractive have not been granted sanctuary. The feeling of being pushed outside the circle of acceptability is not just in the imagination; it represents a very harsh reality. Social discrimination against the overweight is prevalent in all aspects of life, from employment to relationships.

Cartoonist Gary Larson used a *Far Side* comic strip to depict a group of "overeaters anonymous" tourists whose combined weight snaps off the face of the cliff from which they are taking photographs. The caption says "Group Photo Disasters."[5] He would never have been able to publish the cartoon if ethnicity or gender had been the object of his humor. (Unfortunately it's a funny cartoon or I'd really be upset.) But it's one thing to chuckle at humor directed towards a group of which you are a member. It is another thing to have Coach K shout in front of your teammates, "Hey, Hawks, maybe if you lost a little weight you could run faster. You better lay off the milkshakes, boy."

Amid such discrimination and hardship, obesity and unattractiveness become conditions to be devoutly avoided. But as the definition for "acceptable thinness" deviates ever further from the norm, more and more people are getting news from their mirrors that they are now second-rate. Most take the news about as well as the wicked queen. Periodic surveys published in *Psychology Today* have found that body dissatisfaction is rising in the United States and that the rate is accelerating. In 1972, only 25 percent of survey respondents indicated that they were dissatisfied with their body. By 1985, the percentage of those dissatisfied had risen to 38 percent, and by 1997 it was 56 percent.[6] Not only are the numbers of those going to war with the looking glass increasing, but their odds of gaining victory are getting slimmer.

Deeper Implications

Through quizzing hundreds of students at weight-management workshops, it has become clear that students want to lose weight for the same primary reasons: (1) to enhance appearance, (2) to gain love and acceptance, and (3) to increase self-esteem. For a long time I thought about these three responses, and I wondered how they were related. I also wondered how much of an impact these things had on the general life satisfaction of women. At last a clue came from an unexpected direction.

For reasons that I will not bore the reader with, my wife one day handed me a copy of James Dobson's classic *What Wives Wish Their Husbands Knew About Women*.[7] Near the beginning of the book Dr. Dobson introduces the top ten reasons, according to his informal surveys, that women experience depression and unhappiness. He emphasizes that "fully one-third of the group ranked three items within the top five (*Low Self-Esteem; Loneliness, Isolation, and Boredom;* and *Absence of Romantic Love in Marriage*). The women were saying in effect: (1) I don't like myself; (2) I have no meaningful relationships outside my home; and (3) I am not even close to the man I love."

It was easy to find this passage because the page was dog-eared, the lines were highlighted, and the penciled notation in the margin said, "*READ THIS!!*" (How could this have any significance for me? I wondered.)

THE EVIL CHAIN OF ASSUMPTIONS

Even though I couldn't work out the details on my own, I knew that what my wife had shared with me was intimately connected with the reasons that the students in my classes wanted to lose weight. Incapable of solving the mystery myself, I took advantage of the next meeting of my weight-control class to explore the issue. We started out by generating the usual list of why women want to lose weight: appearance, acceptance, and self-esteem. As a separate exercise, I then began to probe the class about those things that caused women the most unhappiness. I was curious to see if I could duplicate Dr. Dobson's findings. "Now then, why are you unhappy?" I asked my students with concern.

My approach was perhaps a bit too rushed and unrefined. After a few moments someone finally said, "Maybe we *are* happy."

"Oh," I said. There was nothing in Dr. Dobson's book about happy women, so I wasn't sure which direction to take the discussion from there. Finally, with a pleading look, I said, "Well, if you weren't happy, then why wouldn't you be?"

Trying to be good sports, the students finally helped me out. At last several answers come forward: "time, children, money, stress," etc. But it was not long before the three reasons cited by Dr. Dobson had been listed at the top of the board: self-esteem, loneliness, and lack of romance. "You know," a student named Carol commented, "when you come right down to it, those three reasons really get to the heart of the matter. Other things may be a hassle, but those are really important." Carol was a middle-aged, married woman who reflected maturity and experience in her answer. Dr. Dobson had come through after all.

I nodded wisely and shared with the students the research of Dr. Dobson, along with his conclusions. I then listed the three primary reasons that women want to lose weight, next to the three reasons that women are most unhappy. While pretending that I knew the answer, I then posed the question I was hoping to understand myself. "So, how do 'reasons women want to lose weight' relate to 'reasons women are unhappy'?"

No one answered the question. The tension finally grew until I had to ask again. "So what do these two lists have in common?" I wondered if I was going to fail in my attempt to uncover and comprehend this mysterious and complex relationship. Once again, my pleading expression of helplessness was not lost on the kind students.

A very thoughtful and reflective young woman named Sarah finally said, "Dr. Hawks, they are essentially the same list."

"Ah," I responded wisely, "of course they are." This bright student then took the chalk from my fingers and approached the board.

"You see," Sarah continued, "it goes something like this"—and then she wrote the words "When I Look Good, Then I'll Be Happy" above the two lists that I had already scrawled on the board.

She then began to draw arrows as she gave the following explanation: "The thinking goes something like this: If I look good then others will be attracted to me. If I am attractive I will be lovable, acceptable, and worthwhile. If I am worthwhile and lovable, then I will find love and acceptance. I will be valued. As a valued person, I will find romance. Romance will be mine! Good-bye loneliness and

---

When I Look Good, Then I'll Be Happy

Reasons to Lose Weight   **Reasons for Unhappiness**

1. Enhance Appearance (Attractiveness)   1. Low Self-Esteem

2. Gain Love and Acceptance   2. Loneliness and Isolation

3. Boost Self-Esteem   3. Lack of Romance

---

isolation. I will feel good about myself. I will have self-esteem. And then I will be happy! (If only I could look good.) That is how the two lists relate to each other.

"What it really represents," Sarah concluded as she handed the chalk back, "is an Evil Chain of Assumptions that keeps us going in a vicious circle. Trying to look good can become the organizing principle around which our unhappy lives revolve."

For a moment I forgot to pretend that *I* was the one who really knew what was going on here. "Wow," I said, "I think you may be right." More to myself than anyone else, I continued, "The chain of assumptions takes into account many of the reasons that women want to lose weight and many of the reasons that they are unhappy. Both the beginning of the problem and the end solution are centered on having the right appearance. The chain of assumptions makes a circle."

To prove this point I took the chalk and drew a circular representation of the Evil Chain of Assumptions, suggested by Sarah.

DENOUNCING THE EVIL CHAIN OF ASSUMPTIONS

"If only we could get off square one," an attractive girl named Brittany laments. "Everything depends on looking good, but the criteria for looking good just keep getting further away from the reality we see reflected every morning in the bathroom mirror." Brittany, a former prom queen, is convinced that being attractive is the key to happiness. For her, the Evil Chain of Assumptions contains no element of evil at all. Instead, it is merely a factual representation of the path to personal fulfillment and happiness. That I had written *evil* as a descriptor for this chain of assumptions does little to deter her from the goal of enhancing personal attractiveness as the first step in making progress toward acceptability. In her estimation, the only thing evil about the chain is that it's getting increasingly difficult to obtain the right appearance.

Brittany is not alone in her thinking. One survey found that 11 percent of women would sacrifice five years of their life to be thin. The same survey found that 24 percent of women would sacrifice three years of their life to be thin.[8] Presumably the sacrificed years of life would be the last few, taken from decrepit old age when they would be feeble and unattractive anyway. But I can only hope that when they reach those later years they will have found something that will make their lives worth living after all, something even more important than having been thin in their youth. Given that thinness is more important than life, it is no wonder that the diet industry has grown to over $50 billion per year.[9]

DARE TO STRIKE OUT AND FIND NEW GROUND

I can't stand the inconsistency any longer. Surely years of precious life are more valuable than thinness. I take out a pair of black-rimmed glasses and put them on. I am instantly transformed from a mediocre, absent-minded professor into an enthusiastic teacher who is passionate about his cause. In my best effort to imitate Jonathan Keating, as performed by Robin Williams in *Dead Poets' Society,* I carefully crawl up on the desk at the front of the class.

Once safely in position, I ask the students with emotion, "Why do I stand up here?"

I can see the answer "Good question!" written in their eyes, but no one says anything. And so I energetically continue.

"I stand upon my desk to remind myself that we must constantly look at things in a different way. You see, the world looks very different from up here. You don't believe me? Take a look for yourselves."

No one moves.

"Just when you think you know something, you have to look at it in another way," I implore. "Even though it may seem silly or wrong, you must try. Now, don't just consider what others think; consider what you think. You must strive to find your own voice. The longer you wait to begin, the less likely you are to find it at all. Thoreau said, 'Most men lead lives of quiet desperation.' Don't be resigned to that. Dare to strike out and find new ground."

After my speech is finished, I quietly step down from the desk, put the glasses away, and resume the mild-mannered demeanor of an ordinary professor. "I do not know how to explain it," I begin, "but I am convinced that the chain of assumptions we have placed on the board is wrong. In other words, I do not believe that by virtue of achieving 'the right appearance' you will increase your sense of acceptability, love, romance, self-worth, or happiness by one iota."

Brittany, the prom queen, looks at me like I have just made a solemn declaration that the sun actually rises in the west. She has been very unimpressed with my impromptu performance. But I will not be intimidated.

"We would do well to follow the counsel of Mr. Keating," I continue. "The Evil Chain of Assumptions represents what *others* think. It is the prevailing wisdom of our society. But we have to consider what *we* think. We have to dare to look at things in a *different* way. I genuinely believe that this chain of assumptions is *evil*. Appearance is *not* the key to realizing our deepest dreams."

Carol, the middle-aged housewife, looks at me intently. Her look says, "Go on, you've just made a strong point—now back up your statement." But I don't know how to back it up, so I just look intently back at her.

Again, Sarah feels compelled to compensate for my lack of understanding. "If appearance becomes the prerequisite first step that leads up the staircase of happiness," she begins slowly, "then that means that we are at the mercy of society to first define which characteristics of appearance are most desirable. We are then compelled to live our lives in a frustrating and often fruitless attempt to measure up to that standard. We are never allowed to define our own standards or to design our own staircase to happiness. If the social standard of beauty is immodest, then we compromise our modesty. If looking good implies certain attitudes and behaviors, then we justify false values (at least values that are false to us). We never realize who we really are. Our vision is clouded, our future is threatened, and our true self is cheapened. Our identity is lost. And all for the sake of living up to standards of beauty that we don't believe in and that will never deliver the love, acceptance, esteem, and happiness that they promise."

As Sarah finishes, I raise my eyebrows knowingly and look back at Carol as if to say, "See, there really is something to what I was saying." Carol nods back. She is thinking deeply about what Sarah just said. But Brittany has long since nodded off. As a class, we are definitely not on the same page. There is much more ground to cover.

That night I take flowers home to my wife and tell her that I love her. She, the students in my class, and Dr. Dobson are slowly teaching me.

SPIRITUAL SOLUTIONS

The Book of Mormon teaches valuable lessons about being pushed outside the circle of love due to appearance. Lesson number one is that if you don't "look right" there will be genuine persecution. You really do get pushed out. Just as we have discussed some of the ways in which the obese and unattractive are discriminated against in our day, the prophet Alma talks of the unattractive who were so mistreated in his day: "For behold, they were cast out of the synagogues because of the coarseness of their apparel. . . . Yea, they were esteemed by their brethren as dross" (Alma 32:2–3).

But lesson number two is even more important: being persecuted on the basis of appearance cannot prevent peace and happiness. Alma "beheld with great joy . . . that their afflictions had truly humbled them, and that they were in a preparation to hear the word" (Alma 32:6). He said to them, "I behold that ye are lowly in heart; and if so, blessed are ye" (Alma 32:8).

In fact, we can set aside the desire to "look good" altogether. "And they did not wear costly apparel, yet they were neat and comely; . . . and thus they began to have continual peace again, notwithstanding all their persecutions, . . . having no respect to persons" (Alma 1:27, 28, 30). By setting aside our battle with the mirror and the quest for unattainable beauty, and instead accepting ourselves for who we are and being neat and comely, we can find peace even in the midst of persecution.

SUMMARY

The rate of body dissatisfaction is increasing dramatically in the United States and other developed countries. This is probably due to changing standards of beauty that deviate ever further from the norm, especially in terms of body size. The pressure to be thin and attractive is also heightened due to very real economic, social, and educational consequences. Political correctness has yet to grant sanctuary to the obese and unattractive.

The reasons that women want to lose weight are directly related to the reasons that they experience unhappiness and depression. In brief, there is an implicit chain of assumptions in our society that the "right" appearance will automatically lead to acceptability, love, romance, self-esteem, and happiness. Obtaining the right appearance has become more important than years of life, and in consequence the weight-loss and beauty industries account for billions of dollars of sales each year.

But as Mr. Keating of *Dead Poet's Society* counsels, we must challenge the socially constructed chain of assumptions because the chain of assumptions is wrong. It is *evil*. The right appearance will not obtain for us any of the other things in the chain. On the other hand, preoccupation with how we look (continually asking the mirror if we are the fairest in the land) can lead to compromised values, standards, and morals, and most important, to a loss of self-identity. Such a pre-occupation also represents a tremendous waste of time and energy that could be devoted to other pursuits with far better results.

Individuals have always been persecuted by the proud and haughty for not living up to social standards of attractiveness. And yet, there can still be happiness. By setting aside our battle with the mirror and the quest for beauty, we can find peace even in the midst of persecution.

CHAPTER THREE

THE INVERTED PYRAMID

The desire of happiness in general is so natural to us that all the world
is in pursuit of it; all have the one end in view, though they take such
different methods to attain it.
—Benjamin Franklin

We begin the next session of our weight-loss class by reading the
following words from the concluding pages of Theodore Dreiser's classic novel *Sister Carrie*.

"And now Carrie had attained that which in the beginning
seemed life's object . . . gowns and carriage, her furniture and bank
account . . . friends who would bow at her success . . . applause . . .
beauty also—and yet she was lonely."[1]

"Carrie," I explain, "is 'an impressionable, Midwestern heroine
hurled into the throbbing, amoral world of the big city.'[2] She believes
with all her heart in the ability of the Evil Chain of Assumptions to
bring her happiness. She claws her way along each link of the chain
until she has mastered them all. But she still ends up lonely and
unhappy.

"Can you assemble all the links in the Evil Chain of Assumptions
and not end up with the final link of happiness?" I ask the class. "Can
an energetic, young life be wasted away in trying to obtain that which
is ultimately of no worth? Or do such unlikely endings occur only in
the world of fictional characters such as Carrie? It seems important to
find answers to such questions."

MASLOW'S HIERARCHY OF NEEDS

"Dr. Hawks," Kristen says, "it seems to me that many of the things that we have been talking about—love and acceptance, self-esteem, and so forth—fit right into Maslow's Hierarchy of Needs. Do you think there's a relationship?"

Kristen, a single woman in her late 20s, works as a nurse at a nearby hospital. She is currently taking a health psychology class and is astute in noting the similarities between our ongoing discussion and Dr. Maslow's theoretical hierarchy of human needs. Kristen is a bright student who has great desires to save humanity, and she is committed to the art of nursing as the proper means for accomplishing the task. As we speak of obesity and health, she makes us toe the line in addressing current biomedical theories as part of our discussion. The result is not always satisfactory to her, but in the case of Abraham Maslow we are in agreement.

Abraham Maslow created a hierarchy of needs that he used to explain the necessary steps that precede self-actualization.[3] The model looks something like this:

MASLOW'S HIERARCHY OF NEEDS

His personal estimate was that only two percent of the population ever achieves self-actualization at the top of the pyramid. He believed that the reason for the 98 percent failure rate is that most people never fully meet the foundational needs of acceptance and self-esteem (shaded in the figure). These are the needs upon which self-actualization is based, and without their supporting strength, actualization is not a realistic possibility. These unmet needs are also closely related to the reasons that women say they want to lose weight and the reasons that women say they are unhappy or depressed.

As envisioned by Maslow, self-actualization represents the pinnacle human need, the realization of which is characterized by developing and expressing innate potential. The concepts of personal fulfillment, life satisfaction, and happiness are intimately connected to the process of self-actualization. Unfortunately, instead of focusing on self-actualization, many of us spend our entire lives trying to find solutions for the lower level needs of loneliness (absence of love and acceptance) and feelings of inadequacy (low self-esteem).

One only needs to reconsider the Evil Chain of Assumptions from the last chapter to understand why many get lost on false paths that never allow them to escape the black cloud of despair that blocks feelings of acceptability and self-worth. It is all about appearance. We think that obtaining the right appearance is the ultimate solution. The Evil Chain of Assumptions says that if we only look "right," then we will find love and acceptance, and self-esteem, etc. But it is getting harder and harder to look good.

MASLOW AND THE EVIL CHAIN OF ASSUMPTIONS

It seems ironic that the links in the Evil Chain of Assumptions, a false path to happiness, seem to share so much in common with Maslow's Hierarchy of Needs, a far more useful path. It is a relationship worth exploring. Since it was her idea, I ask Kristen, the nurse, to come up to the front of the class and diagram the Evil Chain of Assumptions as it might relate to Maslow's Hierarchy of Needs. She's used to telling me how things really are, so this task holds little intimidation for her. She draws the following figure on the board and then offers an explanation.

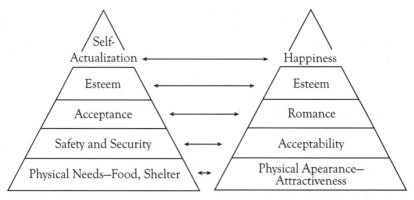

MASLOW'S HIERARCHY OF NEEDS   EVIL CHAIN OF ASSUMPTIONS

"It's like this," she begins, "appearance, the focal 'link' in the Evil Chain of Assumptions, is part of our physical nature—so it goes on the bottom directly across from Maslow's other physical needs. They both provide the prerequisite foundation upon which all the other elements must rest. In the Evil Chain of Assumptions, a sense of acceptability becomes the source of safety and security, and so it goes across from Maslow's safety and security. Romance, on the one side, and love and acceptance, on Maslow's side, are the same concept." She suddenly giggles and blushes at this explanation. (I wink at the rest of the class. It is common knowledge that she recently became engaged.) Eventually, she regains her composure and continues.

"The concept of self-esteem is equivalent on both sides, so they go together," she says as she draws an arrow between the two. "And, as I understand it," she concludes, "Maslow's ideal of self-actualization represents the development and expression of inner potential with a resulting sense of peace and deep satisfaction. Even though the term *happiness* within the Evil Chain of Assumptions may have a different connotation, I think they are similar in that they both represent the highest levels of fulfillment, and both are at the pinnacle of their respective pyramids." She draws the final arrow between these two concepts, and then hands me the chalk on the way back to her seat.

THE INVERTED PYRAMID

At the conclusion of Kristen's presentation, a shy young woman named Holly raises her hand. Holly doesn't say much in class, but she pays very close attention to all that is said. She never makes a comment without first raising her hand and waiting to be called on, but when she does she definitely has something to say. For Holly to speak up in class usually requires a substantial degree of emotional arousal on her part, and apparently Kristen has hit one of Holly's hot buttons.

"Yes, Holly."

"I think that what Kristen has said makes a lot of sense," she begins timidly, "but I think there might be a better way to diagram the Evil Chain of Assumptions in relation to Maslow's hierarchy." Holly is quite overweight, more so than anyone else in the class, and she is very self-conscious about being an overweight person in a weight-loss course. (I have always been surprised by the number of people who approach me and say that they really wanted to take my weight-control course, but were too embarrassed because they were overweight.)

"Would you be willing to offer an alternate diagram?" I ask. I know how much Holly hates to draw attention to herself, and asking her to come to the front of the room and write on the chalkboard is taking a risk. At the same time, I really want to give her the opportunity to stand up and define herself by the quality of her ideas, as opposed to always holding back and being judged by the size of her body.

She realizes the implications of the request and takes a moment before replying. Finally she says, "Well, what I was thinking really wasn't that much different. I think what Kristen drew is probably pretty close to what I was going to draw. Never mind."

Carol, a married, middle-aged mother of three, won't let it rest. "Come on, Holly," she says with the voice of maturity. "I really want to see what you had in mind."

Holly blushes bright red, and beads of sweat stand out on her forehead before she's able to respond. "All right," she finally mutters, and she moves to the front of the room. She is so breathless with emotion and embarrassment that she can hardly speak, so instead she starts drawing.

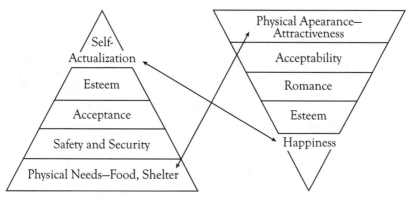

MASLOW'S HIERARCHY OF NEEDS   EVIL CHAIN OF ASSUMPTIONS

"In some ways," she is at last able to say, "the Evil Chain of Assumptions is a distortion of Maslow's hierarchy. The way Kristen drew it, there is a one-to-one correlation between the links of the chain and Maslow's needs. It makes the path of the flawed assumptions look as legitimate as Maslow's hierarchy. But what the Evil Chain of Assumptions actually does is pervert Maslow's hierarchy. It turns it upside down."

"In Maslow's hierarchy, you first meet the basic needs of hunger (a physical need), and then you can move on to the next level of safety, and then once that's met you worry about love and acceptance, and so forth. With the Evil Chain of Assumptions, you don't do things in single steps. You try to do it all in a single leap. You pursue 'the right appearance' (a physical thing) as if it were the highest level human need—just like Carrie in the story."

"And so 'attractiveness' is at the top of an inverted pyramid, and your obsession with getting to the top prevents you from understanding and addressing in proper order all of the other issues—like love, self-esteem, loneliness, and romance—that lie below the great passion for beauty. You just figure that if you can scale the inverted pyramid and finally stand at the top, everything down below will automatically take care of itself. Love, self-esteem, and romance will all happen with no further effort. And all of the pain that goes with not having those things will vanish."

At this point she erases Maslow's hierarchy and leaves the inverted pyramid of evil assumptions by itself. "You see," she continues, "because the pyramid is upside down, there are no steps to the top. It's too top heavy, and there's no way up. The more you throw yourself against the pyramid, trying to jump to the top or trying to dig your fingernails into something that will let you climb, the more unstable it becomes. Eventually it topples over and all your efforts have been worthless." EVIL CHAIN OF ASSUMPTIONS TOPPLES

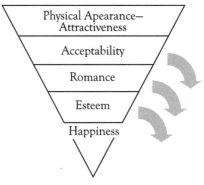

"Even if you're superwoman and can leap to the top in a single bound, your extra weight will just knock it off balance and make it fall over anyway," offers Carol.

"Happiness," says Sarah (the introspective genius of the class), "is now at the bottom of the pyramid. The weight of our obsession with getting the right appearance crushes our chances for real happiness. The upside-down pyramid crushes happiness and smashes it flat."

"And usually it smashes you flat in the bargain," concludes Kristen, the nurse.

As the comments die down, Holly is left standing alone at the front of the room in silence. For a moment, she (and everyone else) forgets to focus on the fact that she is a large woman. She is just a regular person who had something very important to say.

According to Maslow, the first four levels of the hierarchy are called "deficit needs." That is, they are like voids that need to be filled. We can think of them as locks in a canal that need to be filled in order to lift us up to the next level. And then when that new level is filled we continue upward. Like Holly explained, the Evil Chain of Assumptions turns the pyramid upside down, and any reserves that might have built up within the locks of our "deficit" needs just run out. And the void remains impossible to fill. That's why if we ever make it to the top of the inverted pyramid and achieve the crown of attractiveness, it can never fill the void that remains for the rest of our needs.

As opposed to the lower-level "deficit needs," the need for self-actualization is referred to by Maslow as a "being need." Once all the deficit needs have been met, then the need of "being" is met through the realization and expression of unique inner potential. The locks that represent all the deficit needs have filled from within and lift you to the top of the pyramid, and now they must overflow and pour out in order to satisfy the *being* need of self-actualization. The fleeting gratification of *external* accomplishments such as "gowns and carriages, furniture and bank accounts, . . . friends who bow at [your] success, . . . applause, . . . and beauty" can never be an adequate substitute for the deep satisfaction that accompanies the fulfillment of inner needs that finally well up and burst forth in the highest expressions of human potential.

But such is the flawed thinking that leads many of us to believe that by leaping to the top of the inverted pyramid and winning the prize of beauty, we will with the same motion meet the needs of love, acceptance, and self-esteem. In reality they will merely have been bypassed and left unmet. In short, "external obtaining" cannot satisfy the needs of "internal being." And that is why Sister Carrie was still lonely.

SPIRITUAL SOLUTIONS

The wearing of "fine apparel" is consistently used in the Book of Mormon to signify pride and vanity, the division of the population into classes, and the persecution of the poor. The wearing of fine apparel also symbolizes the same unhealthy orientation toward beauty that is portrayed by the inverted pyramid of Maslow.

Speaking directly to us, the prophet Mormon says, "Behold, I speak unto you as if ye were present, and yet ye are not. But behold, Jesus Christ hath shown you unto me, and I know your doing. And I know that ye do walk in the pride of your hearts; and there are none save a few only who do not lift themselves up in the pride of their hearts, unto the wearing of very fine apparel" (Mormon 8:35, 36).

It is not insignificant that Mormon first describes his vision of our day in terms of being lifted up in pride and the wearing of very fine apparel. Mormon saw us accurately. Indeed, there are very few among us who have not tried to climb the upside-down pyramid of Maslow in order to gratify our pride through the realization of beauty—even while neglecting more meaningful pursuits.

We have much to lose if we give in to this orientation. Mormon says, "For behold, ye do love money, and your substance, and your fine apparel . . . more than ye love the poor and the needy. . . . Why do ye adorn yourselves with that which hath no life, and yet suffer the hungry, and the needy, and the naked, and the sick and the afflicted to pass by you, and notice them not? . . . Behold, the sword of vengeance hangeth over you" (Mormon 8:37–41). As cautioned by

Mormon, we must be careful to address the needs for love and acceptance, self-esteem, and self-actualization without inverting Maslow's pyramid and thereby developing an orientation toward appearance that is destructive and futile.

SUMMARY

Maslow's hierarchy represents a logical progression of human needs. As lower level needs are met, they provide a foundation or a stepping stone that enables the individual to concentrate on the next level of needs. Deceptively, the Evil Chain of Assumptions has many similarities with Maslow's hierarchy. They both include physical aspects of our nature, needs for love and acceptance, a desire for self-esteem, and some type of fulfillment which represents the pinnacle of their respective pyramids.

But upon closer examination, the Evil Chain of Assumptions is a perverted form of Maslow's hierarchy. All other needs are set aside and largely ignored while the bulk of attention goes toward the master passion of obtaining the right appearance. As such, it is an inverted pyramid with attractiveness at the top but no steps to get there. It is poorly balanced, poised to fall, and its weight is crushing all of the real needs below it. All of the effort that is expended in trying to climb the inverted pyramid is ultimately wasted as the pyramid eventually falls over or collapses beneath its own weight.

The first four needs of Maslow's hierarchy (Food and Shelter, Safety and Security, Acceptance, Esteem) are like empty vessels that need to be filled. If we turn the pyramid upside down in order to focus on attractiveness as the highest goal, then whatever reserves we may have already applied toward the satisfaction of our true needs is drained and lost. External achievements such as wealth, beauty, or material success can never take the place of inner fulfillment, which provides the foundation for self-actualization.

The wearing of "fine apparel" is consistently used in the Book of

Mormon to signify pride and vanity, the division of the population into classes, and the persecution of the poor. It also represents the destructive orientation that is reflected by the inverted pyramid of Maslow. Even though it is a difficult task, we must find ways to meet our emotional and spiritual needs that do not rely on the supposed merits of achieving the right appearance.

IN SEARCH OF LOVE AND ACCEPTANCE

The most immediate motivation behind our desire to remedy the imperfections that we find reflected in the mirror is the belief that our appearance determines the likelihood that our need for love and acceptance will be met. However, our previous analyses of the Evil Chain of Assumptions and Maslow's inverted pyramid have revealed our misplaced emphasis on physical attractiveness as the key for meeting this vital need.

Section two attempts to clarify the real nature of our need for love and acceptance, and it also depicts the primary strategies that we generally employ in our pursuit of love. It critically evaluates each strategy and makes recommendations in relation to a sure path for meeting the very real need that we all have to feel loved. This section also makes clear the tenuous relationship between appearance and loveability, and the role that love can play in our efforts to make peace with the image in the mirror.

CHAPTER FOUR

LOOKING THROUGH THE EYES OF LOVE

We work so consistently to disguise ourselves to others that we end by being disguised to ourselves.
—François, Duc de La Rochefoucauld

I can remember too many times in my life when I missed out on love because I felt unworthy of it. Growing up in Moab, Utah, my first girlfriend was Monica, literally the girl next door. We were born one day apart at the local hospital, and by the time we were in first grade it was romance. The only problem was the way that the budding fondness was expressed. She would chase me at recess, and I would run away. I felt too awkward to interact with her, so I just ran while she chased me. And I kept running. I had the deepest crush on her all through school, but the romance never recovered from my sense of ineptitude. I still feel awkward whenever I see Monica to this day.

It was not that love and friendship were unavailable; it was my sense of inadequacy that blocked the ability to feel the love that was being expressed. I was too preoccupied with thinking about how dumb or unattractive I was to ever turn my attention to the affection that was being offered. How many friendships and romances have we foregone because of a critical inner gaze that detracts from them and incapacitates us?

Together with the members of my weight-loss class I began to explore ways to deal with this sense of inadequacy. This chapter reveals our attempts to arrive at new insights, and it exposes the *wrong* way to deal with feelings of low self-worth.

A CRITICAL INNER GAZE

The year is 1812. We are in Moscow, and the armies of Napolean are waging war all around us. I play the part of Pierre, a wealthy young prince whose brief experiences on the battlefield have changed him from a callous playboy into a reflective and deeply passionate philosopher.

Holly, the timid student in my class, plays the part of Natasha, a young woman who has been disappointed in love.

"Pierre," I explain to the class, "comes to love Natasha more than life. He hopes to comfort her; he has already been inspired by her."

Holly and I are dressed for our parts in the garb of Russian nobility. As class begins I kneel before the beautiful Natasha:

"But one thing I beg of you," I say fervently as I look up into her eyes, "consider me your friend. If you want help, or advice, or simply to open your heart to someone—think of me."

"But—," Holly slowly replies, "—but, *I am not worthy.*"

At this point the play-acting pauses, and I stand up before the class and repeat the words "*Not worthy?* Natasha says she's not worthy, and therefore earnest Pierre is rebuked. Why, I ask, is she not worthy?"

Not being familiar with the story of Tolstoy's *War and Peace,* from which this scene is taken, the students manufacture reasons that Natasha might feel unworthy to respond favorably to Pierre's declarations of affection.

"Maybe she has some hidden secret from her past that she's trying to hide," offers Brittany.

"Or maybe she loves someone else," says Kristen (the nurse who has a fiancé). As soon as she says this she turns bright red, and everyone smiles indulgently in her direction. She can't even *say* the word *love* without completely losing control of her facial color. Her emotions have never been far from the surface since her recent engagement.

"She might think that she's not pretty enough," whispers Holly, the overweight student who is painfully conscious of her perceived shortcomings in this area. (The fact that Holly was willing to play the part of Natasha, however, is good.)

"She's not really rejecting him," explains Matthew, the one male in the class and the only student who is genuinely taking the class because he 'just needs one extra credit.' "She is playing the old cat-and-mouse game, trying to string him along. She wants to hear him beg before she'll give in." Usually when Matthew offers his opinions, the other members of the class give him an annoyed look, then shake their heads back and forth, and roll their eyes. In response to this comment he gets the usual treatment.

Coming to Matthew's rescue, I step up and explain. "Natasha was reluctant to receive Pierre's declarations of love for the very reason that she gave him: she simply didn't feel worthy of being loved, by him or by anybody. If we don't *think* we are worthy of being loved, then it is difficult to *feel* the love and acceptance that others express for us. So, what must we do to feel love from others? How do we gain love and acceptance as required by Maslow's Hierarchy of Needs, especially if we feel unworthy of it? What will make us feel worthy of the love that others have to offer us?"

I take Holly by the hand and raise her from her seat at the front of the class. "These are the questions that we must answer," I say as I carefully escort the princess back to her seat, "because the answers are important if we are ever to make peace with the mirror. We often hope that this sense of worthiness and acceptance will come automatically when the mirror finally tells us that we are fair enough. But remember the case of the wicked queen from Snow White: the mirror may never let us off the hook—no matter to what extremes we may take our efforts."

Love Is Not a Prize

The frustrating search for feelings of worth, at least as sought from the mirror, may take us in all the wrong directions. In fact, our efforts to generate inner worth by creating outer beauty may actually be the most effective way to lock a sense of unworthiness deep inside and forever drive love away—just as Natasha sent Pierre away, and just as I ran from Monica. We are mistaken in the point that inner worth will be the reward of achieving the right appearance. And we are also mistaken in thinking that love will be the ultimate prize, even if we do become attractive, and even if we at last feel worthy of it. Love, I will argue, must already exist before worth is felt.

In our personal war with the looking glass, the concept of love lies at the center of the battlefield. We begin the war with high hopes of obtaining love as part of the victor's crown. But rather than being the reward of victory, perhaps love should be one of the primary weapons with which we fight the war. Until we understand and act upon this concept, love becomes the sticking point. We think that the war is fought to get love, and yet the war cannot be won without already having love on our side. We confuse the end with the means. The end for which we strive is greater than love, but love is the means by which we must advance in the great struggle with the mirror. Love is not the prize we fight for, it is the bright sword we brandish as we fight.

"But how can we have love on our side, how can we wield it like a sword if we don't feel that other people love us? Especially if we feel like Natasha, that we aren't even lovable?" This question is raised by Holly, and she is sincere in her desire to find an answer.

THE FALLACY OF TRYING TO CREATE A LOVABLE FAÇADE

By now I have learned the fallacy of asking students about the *personal* motivations that drive their behavior. Since our own motivations are invariably pure, an analysis of them is unrevealing. And so instead I ask them, "How do *other* people generally try to develop the sense of worth that will allow them to receive love and acceptance from those around them?"

Up to this point, the introspective and thoughtful Sarah has been very quiet. Sarah is thin, quite tall, and an academic genius. Often when she answers a question, the depth of her insights is beyond reach. At the same time, Sarah has little in the way of a social life. Her intelligence perhaps makes her intimidating to other students, and she is most often left to herself. Every time I look at Sarah, I think of the heroine of Patricia MacLachlan's novel *Sarah, Plain and Tall*. A noble woman with much to offer, and yet tall and plain.

Before anyone else can answer, Sarah demonstrates that she has been paying attention to the discussion. "We mostly try to guess what other people want us to be like," she says, "and then we try to be that way. To put it in more negative terms, we try to create a façade that we think will be sufficient to inspire the love and acceptance within others that we desire to obtain from them. We may seek to win approval by trying to be pretty or cute or clever—or," and she makes this last comment very quietly, "—or by trying to appear smart."

"Let's take the case of Aladdin," I offer. "My little daughter Jessica was three when the Disney version of *Aladdin* came out. We immediately purchased the video when it was released. Jessica watched it 1,379 consecutive times." (Together we memorized it, and once again I discovered insights that could be applied to our conflict with the mirror.)

"When Aladdin is at the bottom of Princess Jasmine's tower, he asks the genie how he can win her love. The genie encourages him to "tell the truth," but for Aladdin the truth is that he is a lowly street rat, completely unworthy of the love of the princess. He insists that the pretense of a suave and debonair prince will serve him better than the 'truth.' But with what result does the sophisticated prince woo the beautiful princess?"

"Jasmine tries to push him off the tower," Kristen answers with a smile.

The Two Evils of Rejection and Acceptance

"We will encounter one of two results when we try to win love and acceptance by putting up a false front," I continue. "We will either be rejected out of hand, like Aladdin, or we will be accepted on the merits of the façade. Which is worse?"

Sarah is again quick to offer her thoughts. "If our outer image gets rejected," she explains, "then it's no skin off our nose. Our real self wasn't rejected. We just go back to the drawing board and try to perfect the front so that it will get us accepted the next time. But if we get *accepted* on the merits of our public image, then we are in trouble."

She thinks a moment before continuing. "I may not have seen *Aladdin* quite as many times as your daughter, but I know that Jasmine finally buys into Aladdin's charade and that a lot of the movie is about his anxiety over being exposed. To be accepted because of a façade is to be accepted because of the quality of your deception. The implication is a lifetime of effort devoted to the maintenance of that deception, all the while fearing discovery and rejection as an unworthy charlatan. In the meantime, the preoccupation with maintenance of the veneer prevents the real you from ever being explored or developed. The true self is sacrificed on a false errand, and the *real* you never receives genuine love and acceptance." This Sarah, plain and tall is full of character and insight that transcend her physical features.

Carol, who has lived a full life, raised a family, and devoted her life to one man, gives her a mature perspective: "If you are accepted as a façade, then you are basically being accepted as an object whose primary purpose is to become a source of gratification for someone else. Your value is measured in terms of *usefulness*, in much the same way that a broom's value is measured. As long as it fulfills its assigned task at an acceptable level, keep it. Once it doesn't sweep very well anymore, throw it away. As an object you are disposable when your *usefulness* is no longer needed. No one worries about how a broom feels when it gets tossed, and no one will worry about how you feel when you are dismissed."

The recently engaged Kristen has been frightened by such talk. "Let me get this straight. Do you mean to tell me that if a man primarily likes you because you're attractive, that he's basically interested in using you as an object to gratify his ego and lust? And that he will get rid of you like an old shoe once he finds a new object that can do a better job?" The rest of the class offers smiles of sympathetic kindness, but no one refutes her assertion.

THE BETTER THE FAÇADE, THE LONELIER THE PERSON

"Michael," I ask, "how do you feel when in the company of a very attractive woman, someone who has an impeccable, made-up image?"

"Very intimidated," he replies. "I normally wouldn't dare talk to her or interact with her. I'd be chicken."

"And how would you feel in the company of such a woman?" I ask prom queen Brittany.

"Jealous and angry," she says without hesitation.

"And so," I summarize, "trying to create the perfect façade in order to feel worthy of receiving love and acceptance may actually lead to increased isolation and loneliness as the façade intimidates, frightens, and enrages others. And not only that, it turns you into an object to be used and discarded at the whim of those you are trying to please—with no thought for your feelings or needs. There is intense pressure to maintain the pretense, and the result is eternal preoccupation with looks. And then, worst of all, when it all fails and comes crashing down, the resulting disappointment and unhappiness are falsely blamed on the inadequacy of the façade, and the painful cycle starts over again. The more emphasis that is placed on the façade as an outward representation of personal value, the more likely that inner feelings of low worth will become permanent."

"Just like the wicked queen from *Snow White*," Holly says. "She tries poison apples and poison combs and does all kinds of wicked things just because the mirror kept telling her that her outer image wasn't good enough. We need to just let it go."

The Terror Behind the Façade

But most of us can't just let it go because then the real, unworthy you is left open to exposure and possible rejection. Just like Aladdin, we fear exposure as worthless street rats. If the wicked queen is not "the fairest in the land," then what's left for her? If all of your life's efforts have gone into creating a perfect façade as a symbol of what's valuable about you, then there has been no development of the real you. You become terrified at the thought of having the outer shell taken away only to reveal the small, undeveloped, frightened person who hides behind it. (Like the little man behind the curtain who is pretending to be the Great Oz.) And so you cling desperately to the hope that the veneer will hold together and do its work—even if you have to pass out a few poison apples along the way. You come to define your worth in terms of the usefulness of the façade. If it fails, you feel worthless because you think there's nothing else to offer.

As a modern example, take the case of Alicia Machado, Miss Universe from Venezuela in 1996. When crowned she was 5'8" tall and weighed 118 pounds (a typical body size for beauty pageant contestants and fashion models). When asked what she was going to do now that she was Miss Universe, she said, "Eat, eat, eat." Apparently she had starved herself down to 118 and was now ready to go off the diet. She quickly made good on her promise and "ballooned" (as the media put it), from 118 all the way up to a "grotesque" 165 pounds. (She claims she never got above 155.) Her weight gain was considered such an insult to the image of beauty that the judges threatened to take away her crown, and her eating and body size became the dominant theme of her reign. *Newsweek* carried a picture of her exercising before a group of photographers. The caption read, "Miss Universe says no to sweets, yes to sweat."[1] She was forced to offer public proof that she was trying to shore up the collapsing façade.

Ironically, the popular opinion seemed to be against Miss Machado. (Yet, less than two percent of females who are 5'8" tall weigh as little as 118 pounds.) This is especially interesting because at the time she was crowned her body mass index was 17.9, which is considered to be underweight and possibly unhealthy due to correlations with osteoporosis, malnutrition, and eating disorders. In a developing country, someone with this low of a body mass index would be included by the World Health Organization in the statistics that describe the number of starving people in the world.

But when Miss Machado "ballooned" up to 165 pounds, her body mass index would have been 25, which is considered to be within the "normal" range for women. And so we have allowed the beauty industry to define attractiveness in a way that is several notches away from normal, at least in terms of a healthy body size. Ballooning all the way up from malnourished to normal, healthy body size was such an affront to elegance that Miss Universe was publicly humiliated and threatened with the loss of her crown. It would be no less ludicrous to demand that beauty queens wear a size 3 shoe or that they have artificially elongated necks. Those who could not comply would be publicly humiliated and drummed out of the competition. With such harsh consequences for nonconformance, and with such unrealistic standards of acceptability, it is small wonder that so many are tormented by feelings of inadequacy and so many keep trying to measure up.

Still upset by some of the points that have come out of this discussion, Kristen earnestly asks the question—"So how do you know if someone really likes *you*, or if he's just in it for the façade?"

I answer her question with one of my own. "Has that someone seen the real you, or has he seen only a façade?"

SPIRITUAL SOLUTIONS—LOOKING THROUGH THE EYES OF LOVE

"But the Lord said unto Samuel, look not on his countenance, or on the height of his stature; . . . for man looketh on the outward appearance, but the Lord looketh on the heart" (1 Samuel 16:7). If only we could feel comfortable interacting with each other at the level of the heart, rather than relying on the pretense of our outward appearance to define our relative worth. Somehow we must learn to overcome our sense of inadequacy without relying on a false front. Otherwise, we are likely to miss out on opportunities for genuine love and friendship.

I once again take Holly by the hand and gently lead her to the throne of the princess at the front of the room. I kneel at her feet.

"But one thing I beg of you," I plead with renewed energy, "consider me your friend. If you want help, or advice, or simply to open your heart to someone—think of me."

"But—," Holly repeats slowly, "—but, *I'm not worthy.*"

"If I were not myself," I proclaim, "but the handsomest, cleverest, and best man in the world, and were free, I would this moment ask on my knees for your hand and for your love."

Holly smiles and squeezes my hand.

After a pause I explain to the class, "Eventually, Natasha is able to overcome her sense of unworthiness and accept the love that Pierre offers her. They have a wonderful life together, happy in the love that they have for each other. May we learn their secret, and in our own lives find the happiness that they found."

Holly feels inadequate because of her size, and Sarah feels inadequate because she is "plain and tall." But I see hope in their eyes as they consider these ideas. It is our sense of unworthiness, often blamed on appearance, that causes us to hide from love even when it is expressed. But if we could look through the eyes of love and behold the worth of the inner soul as seen by the Savior, then our sense of unworthiness would slowly melt away.

And so we return to the earlier point that *we must have love on our side from the beginning.* It is only by seeing our inner heart through the clear eyes of love that we can find our true sense of worth. The more we look for external pegs upon which to hang our sense of worth, the less likely we are to ever discover our true value.

The Lord looks on the heart of men, rather than on their external appearance—perhaps because he is looking through the eyes of love. Just as the Lord does, we must learn to look at our own hearts through the eyes of love, rather than fixing our gaze on the imperfect image in the mirror.

As we try to overcome the tendency to judge ourselves based on appearance and follow the Lord's example of looking at the heart, then we will become more confident in defining our worth without reference to the outer countenance. Once this process is underway, the next step is to overcome our fear of rejection, and then boldly step forward as an authentic person. Only as we interact with others by revealing our true selves can we know that we are accepted for who we really are, not for what we pretend to be.

SUMMARY

If we don't *think* we are worthy of being loved, then it is difficult to *feel* the love and acceptance that others express to us. It is deceptive to think of love as the ultimate prize that we fight for. Instead we should consider love to be our most valuable tool in overcoming our sense of inadequacy as we struggle to make peace with the image in the mirror.

Too often, we try to obtain love and acceptance by creating a façade to inspire the affection of others. But when we try to obtain love by putting up a false front, we are either rejected because of the shallowness of our façade, or we are accepted because of the value that our image has for others. Being accepted is worse because it obligates us to a lifetime of effort devoted to maintaining the illusion, all the while fearing discovery as a charlatan.

In the meantime, the inner person is never explored or developed. The true self is sacrificed, and the *real* you never receives the love that was needed. We come to depend on the façade to represent our worth to others. If it fails, then all is lost. But in the end, just like with the wicked queen, it always fails. Eventually the mirror will tell us that we are no longer fair enough. The resulting unhappiness is wrongly blamed on the inadequacy of our image, and the tragic cycle continues. But the real blame for our unhappiness lies in our method of pursuing love (trying to develop the perfect façade), not with the inadequacy of our appearance.

We are afraid to lay aside our public front because of the very real social consequences that we fear will befall us if our true self is exposed to scrutiny. And yet, it is time to lay the outer shell aside and find a new strategy for getting love on our side—a strategy that does not depend on complicity with the mirror. The Lord looks on the heart of men, rather than on their external appearance. Just as the Lord does, we must learn to look at our own hearts through the eyes of love, and then base our sense of worth on the genuine value that we find there.

CHAPTER FIVE

OVERCOMING THE FEAR OF REJECTION

Be so true to thyself as thou be not false to others.
—Francis Bacon

When Aladdin asked the genie how he could get Princess Jasmine to like him, the genie told him to just "be yourself; tell the truth." In the movie it was obvious that Jasmine liked Aladdin most when she first met him as a resourceful street rat. But when he tried to be a suave prince, she had little use for him. From his perspective it was too great a risk to appear honestly as himself. As himself, he wasn't good enough.

Often the same feelings of doubt prevent us from being ourselves. Like Aladdin, it is our fear of being who we are that may prevent others from knowing the things about us that they might actually like the most. But why are we so afraid to just be who we are? The great fear of rejection has to be demystified and conquered in order to take the next step in making peace with the image in the mirror.

THE FEAR IS BASED ON MYTHS

Having taught at the university level for more than ten years, it has not been unusual for me to have some students take my classes as freshmen, and then as upper-division students, and finally again as graduate students. But I have been surprised to realize that some of these students, after having taken five or six classes from me, had never voluntarily made a single comment in any of my classes. "Why?" I ask my current class of weight-loss students.

"Because they're afraid they'll say something stupid," Brittany answers smugly. Apparently the fear of rejection is not something that she struggles with.

"Exactly," I agree. "But let's examine the assumptions upon which their fear is based. Maybe the risk of appearing honestly as ourselves, and allowing others to see us as we really are (warts and all), isn't such a great risk after all. Aladdin would have been much better off if he would have been honest from the beginning. Maybe the risk of hiding behind an artful façade or behind reclusive anonymity is far riskier— at least in relation to meeting our need for love and acceptance."

Myth Number One: People Notice You

The fear of just letting go and being who we are is based in part on the assumption that someone is actually noticing us and putting forth an effort to make some type of meaningful judgment in relation to what we do or say. We will call this *myth number one*. The reality is that no one is noticing you. Whether this is a disappointment or a relief will depend on your perspective. But it remains a truth.

"Take the students who are afraid to make a comment in class," I explain. "As Brittany pointed out, they are afraid of looking dumb, so they never say anything. But what is going on in the minds of the other students?"

"All the other students are too busy wondering about what everyone thinks of them to worry about what they think of anyone else," Carol says with a smile. "If my life is at all representative of others, then we all spend the biggest part of our lives wondering what other people think of us. So much so, that we don't have any time to devote to thinking about anyone else. We can't pass a mirror or window without tossing our hair and trying to catch our reflection to see how we look. As if there are people out there who aren't already too preoccupied with their *own* looks to take notice of what *we* look like. And so chances are you could say whatever you wanted in class, brilliant or idiotic, and you'd be lucky either way if anyone paid one bit of attention."

Myth Number Two: You Can Know What Others Think

"Let's just suppose," I continue, "that someone actually did notice you. As unlikely as it may be, let's just suppose that someone observed you and arrived at some type of conclusion based on what you have said, or done, or about what you look like. *Myth number two* is that you can somehow know what their perception is. The sad (or happy) reality is that you will never know for sure what they really think about you. No matter how close you are to them, no matter what they say or how sincerely they say it, no matter how disinterested they may seem, and no matter how badly you want to believe or disbelieve what they say, you will never know for sure what they really think about you."

Kristen, with the boyfriend, looks shocked and horrified. "My boyfriend—," she starts and then once again blushes herself into deep crimson, "—my boyfriend told me last night that he really liked how my new dress looks. Are you trying to tell me that I should suspect his sincerity and truthfulness?"

"He might be sincere," I say, "or maybe he's not. Maybe he just loves you. You see, when I come home from work on a night when I have a date planned with my wife and she greets me with a new dress on and then asks me how she looks, I say with deep sincerity and admiration, 'Wow, that dress looks great. I really like it. Let's go.' I say this because I have learned that this is the most likely response to result in a pleasant date. I may actually like the dress, but at the same time I may not particularly care for it. If not, I do not tell her what I really think because if I do (and I have in the past) then there is a strong probability that we will never go on the planned date. Instead we will sit down and process my thoughts about her dress for the rest of the evening. She will be hurt by what I said, and it will take a long time before the wounds of that night heal."

Carol laughs at this explanation, but Kristen is near tears. "But I want to know how he *really* feels," Kristen says. "If he doesn't like my dress, then I want to know about it."

"No you don't," Carol says under her breath.

"I expect complete honesty in our relationship," Kristen continues. "I don't see how anyone could be happy under any other terms."

"First," Carol explains, "he probably wouldn't have noticed that you had on a new dress or taken any other thought about your appearance if you hadn't brought up the issue. *Myth one* really is a myth, especially when it comes to men noticing the things you have done to make yourself look more attractive.

"Second," she continues, "if you really love someone, then you protect their feelings in relation to those things that are not important. It isn't important whether he likes your dress or not, but it does matter that he cares about how you feel about yourself. And so if he tells you that you look nice, even though he may not really think so, then he is a man who feels genuine love for you. He knows that since you went to the trouble to pick out and buy the dress, then you must like it, and that's enough for him. If you are wearing something that will cause people to throw rotten vegetables at you, then he should feel obligated to warn you. But anything short of that should call forth nothing but undying praise, and even the racks should not be able to make him say otherwise."

"According to Dr. James Dobson," I add, "*'honesty that doesn't have the best interest of the hearer at heart is a cruel form of selfishness.'*[1] The bottom line is that in the unlikely event that someone actually perceives us, we will never know for sure what their perception is. No matter how close we are to that person, and no matter how sincerely they express themselves. And since we can never know what they are actually thinking about us, perhaps we shouldn't concern ourselves so much with wondering and worrying about it."

Myth Number Three: We Can Control the Feelings of Others

The most destructive myth of all is that *we* can do things that will determine the feelings that *others* have for us. This is *myth number three*. As a new college professor I desired deeply to be liked by my students and to be perceived by them as a good teacher. And so I tried to imagine what they wanted most in a professor and then tried to live up to that expectation. The result, I felt, should have been unanimous approval from the students in my classes—but it wasn't. Even if the majority of the students were happy with the class, it was devastating when someone was critical. Subsequent efforts to try even harder to measure up to student expectations resulted in even worse evaluations.

In short, there was nothing *I* could do that could control the perceptions that *students* had of my courses. They were in control of what they thought and felt, not I—and there was nothing I could do about it. I had no more luck convincing my students that I was a great teacher than Aladdin had in convincing Jasmine that he was a suave prince.

"Don't let it bother you too much, Dr. Hawks," Sarah says. "We all like you."

This thoughtful comment might have offered some comfort if Brittany could have kept from rolling her eyes as it was being made.

Myth Number Four: Perfection Evokes Love

We watch super athletes receive gold medals and Hollywood stars receive Academy Awards. We see the applause that rock stars receive from a stadium full of crazed fans. And based on these observations we come to believe that those who achieve some level of perfection are able to evoke love and acceptance from others. If we too could perfect some talent or skill, then love and acceptance would come our way. This is *myth number four*.

ONE PERSON'S EXPERIENCE

Take the example of Bette Midler. When she received an award for some type of theatrical achievement, she was quoted as saying, "The worst part of success is trying to find someone who is happy for you."[2] And sadly she's right. We strive all our lives to obtain the love and recognition we think will automatically accompany success and achievement, but the reality is a letdown. For those of us watching her receive the award (assuming someone actually watched), we may think that she is one of the beautiful people who has obtained perfection and love, along with the athletes, rock stars, and other pop culture heroes. But as we use her example to review the myths above, a different possibility unfolds.

No One Notices You. While Bette may have a cadre of true fans, most people couldn't care less about who she is or what she has accomplished with her life. They watch her on a pedestal of glory as she receives her award, then they yawn and look for the remote. She never crosses their minds again.

You Will Never Know What They Think. In relation to those who may actually admire Bette, she will never know for sure who they are or what they really think. Even if there is someone who admires her immensely, chances are that she will never know about or experience a lasting impact from that admiration.

You Can't Control the Feelings of Others. No matter how hard she tries, she will never be able to control how people feel about her. Whether they like or dislike her will always be their choice, regardless of anything she does to try and influence the outcome.

Perfection Is a Repellent. And finally, concerning myth number four, Bette's apparent perfection does little to make us feel close to her. Rather than attract, perfection functions almost as a repellent. She is so high up on her pedestal that we are not likely to call out to her, "Hey girlfriend, you wanna get together this afternoon and put up some tomatoes?" She is too far above us to be considered for the common interactions of mere mortals. Just like Sister Carrie, she may still be lonely even with all of her wealth, popularity, success, and attractiveness.

STRENGTH ALIENATES; WEAKNESS ATTRACTS

It is ironic that we often wish that we could be like the beautiful people so that we too could be happy and loved. But even a cursory look at the lives of the rich and famous reveals a level of unhappiness that is anything but enviable. Achievement, success, recognition, fame, power, and other symbols of "perfection" do not convey love, acceptance, or happiness.[3]

"Even among the people around us," Carol comments in class one day, "we often feel uncomfortable around those who seem most perfect. In many cases it seems that the strengths of others alienate us from them because we feel like they are in a different league. But weaknesses bring us together. We don't feel any sympathy for the apparently flawless person, but we do for the one who is blemished. If someone makes a brilliant comment in class, it reminds us how different they are from us. But if someone blunders, then our heart goes out to them because we have all stepped in the very same cow pie. Our weaknesses and common flaws, when shared openly, create a bond between us. Our strengths and apparent perfections push us apart."

"If someone I know is sad over a shortcoming or a problem they have," Kristen adds, "I will want to hold and comfort them and even share with them similar problems or shortcomings that I have experienced. But if someone comes to me with an attitude of superiority and invulnerability, then I want to turn my back and head the other way.

So if we keep hiding our weaknesses while parading our perfections, we will get the response that is opposite from what we are really seeking."

"And so we're supposed to make dumb comments in class so other people will feel sorry for us?" Sarah asks. I saw her wince at Carol's comment about people who alienate others by making intelligent comments in class.

"Whether we like it or not," I intervene, "we all have strengths, and we all have flaws. But if we use our strengths as a shield behind which to hide our flaws and as a symbol with which to promote our superiority, then they become a liability to us—at least as far as obtaining love and acceptance from others is concerned. As we will discuss later, it turns out that our strengths can be very important to us, depending on how we understand and use them. What we're talking about here is not a call to embrace mediocrity as a path to love. But it is a call to abandon the fear of rejection, which is the underlying reason that we refuse to show our true selves to each other, with both strengths *and* flaws."

I have noticed that social gatherings of people often deteriorate into popularity contests where personal attention is sought by relating the best joke, story, or one-liner. Seldom does the conversation get down to the level of what people really think and feel about things that are dear to them. But it is only by expressing these deeper feelings and ideas that we can experience closeness with others. It's the only way we can gain the sense of comfort that arises from exploring our common struggles, doubts, and inadequacies. The popularity contest, while perhaps entertaining, leaves us feeling isolated.

OVERCOMING THE FEAR

In the final analysis, it seems that the ultimate fuel on which the fear of rejection feeds is the preoccupation with ourself. We are preoccupied with wondering what others think about us, never tired of trying to comprehend the unknowable perceptions of others, and try-ing to think of new ways to control how others feel about us. We are catering to what we think they want us to be like and putting forth our strengths as if they were our defining traits. We are coming up with the best stories or one-liners so that we are the hit of the party, or hiding behind silence and avoiding involvement and engagement with others. But we are always afraid that if others knew what we were like deep down inside, they would reject us. We are in the same boat as Aladdin.

But if no one is really noticing us and if we can never know what they think (even if they were to notice us), and if the things we do cannot control what they think anyway, then we can't really be *rejected* by them. Whether they have feelings of love or rejection towards us is unknowable and uncontrollable; it is therefore unworthy of our time, energy, and anxiety. It's not that we don't care, because we care deeply about what others think about us, but we let go of the concern because it is unknowable and uncontrollable.

What we can do is relinquish the preoccupation with self, and instead put forth the effort to notice others. We can decide what we think about them, and we can exercise control over our own percep-tions of them. And so the real choice that we have is whether or not we accept and appreciate them and what they have to offer. This is the key to overcoming the fear of rejection. We must focus our attention on the decision of whether to accept and appreciate others, rather than drown in a sea of concern about whether others accept and appreciate us.

"There is no reason to fear rejection," I offer by way of conclu-sion. "Most people don't notice us, we can never know what they think if they actually do notice us, and we can't control how they feel anyway. And most often, even if we expose our weaknesses, it will actually make others feel closer to us. In fact, fear of rejection is self-ish. It arises with a preoccupation about *me* and how *I* feel.

PUTTING IT TO THE TEST

Some years ago Steve (my biologist coworker) and I were at a conference in Washington, D.C. As we traveled on the subway system we became engaged in a deep discussion involving many of the points that we have been discussing. "Isn't it interesting," I commented, "that even though there is a universal need for love and acceptance, virtually every passenger on this subway seems to be in their own isolated world—even while being surrounded by thousands and millions of fellow travelers."

"What would happen," Steve asked, "if instead of worrying about what others may or may not be thinking about us, we were to focus our energies on noticing those people around us, and then expressing our sincere perceptions to them?" After debating this question for some time, we decided to seek an answer in the form of an experiment, or rather, a contest. The rules of the contest were simple: (a) focus your attention on a fellow subway rider and form a sincere, positive perception in relation to that person, (b) express your perception to him or her in an open and honest manner, and (c) take notice of the response. No response or a negative response was worth zero points. A smile or kind response was worth 10. A handshake was worth 20, and a pat on the arm was worth 30. A response that took the form of a hug earned an immediate 50 points, while a kiss brought in an automatic 100.

My first traveler was an older woman standing nearby whose unfocused gaze was directed out a darkened window. After turning my full attention on her, I approached and said, "Excuse me, but that hat reminds me of one that my sister likes to wear. Do you mind telling me about it?" At first she was somewhat startled at the intrusion, but once she sensed that my question was sincere she provided me with the natural history of her hat as requested. We then spoke of my sister's hat and how much it meant to her. Our discussion moved to general topics of family, a declaration of common interests, and finally an expression of delight at having met and shared some moments together. I was left with a tender pat on the arm as she stepped off the train at her stop.

Steve and I became so intrigued and enthusiastic with our contest that it lasted for much of the day. It continued as we visited the Smithsonian museums, strolled about the Mall, and returned to our hotel on the subway. We visited with people of all ages, both sexes, many different races, and many nationalities. We both brought in more than 1,000 points.

Before we were finished, our small contest had yielded many insights. The most important was that since most people are burdened with worry about how they are being perceived by others, the unsolicited expression of a sincere, positive perception is received most gladly. It generally led to lively discussions, mutual manifestations of warmth and kindness, and in the end a very friendly parting of the ways (with even a few hugs). And yet, most subway riders stare vacantly ahead, read a book, or sleep—often preoccupied with wonder about what others might be thinking of them, but never once forming or expressing a perception they might have developed of someone else. And thus the loneliness and isolation overwhelm us, while meaningful companionship is only an arm's length away. If only we could overcome the fear of rejection and be the one to step forward first.

SPIRITUAL SOLUTIONS

In his ministry, the Savior did not attempt to gain love and acceptance from others by trying to conform to what he thought they would like. In fact, I don't believe that he tried to gain love and acceptance at all. What he did was call forth all the talents and abilities with which his Father had blessed him, and then use those talents and abilities to bless the lives of others. The result was that some people chose to love and follow him, and some people chose to despise and reject him. For him, the realization of love and acceptance wasn't dependent on how others responded to him. His sense of love and acceptance was based on what he felt for others and on his life of service to them. He did not waste his life trying to please others by conforming to their expectations so that they would like him.

As I have matured as a teacher, I have tried to worry less about trying to be what I assume my students want me to be, and instead have focused on trying to understand and develop whatever it is that I have to offer them as a teacher. Whether the students are satisfied with my offering is their concern, but I am content with knowing that I have put forth my best effort and that my motivation was based on a sincere love for them. Their input and feedback are very important to me, and I care very much about how they feel about my courses. But my primary focus is on giving them the best of the genuine me, which is all I really have to offer. And, ironically, if they want to learn from me, then this is what they want me to be like anyway.

In the last chapter we concluded that we must learn to look at our own heart through the eyes of love, rather than focus our attention on our physical image. In this chapter we have started to learn that we must also focus our attention on the hearts of others as seen through the same eyes of love. If we will do so, then we can overcome the fear of rejection.

Jesus taught us to disregard the sting of rejection from others and to instead focus on our love for them. "But I say unto you, love your enemies, bless them that curse you, do good to them that hate you, and pray for them which despitefully use you, and persecute you" (Matthew 5:44). In the next chapter we will consider the need for love and acceptance as it can be met through our feelings and expressions of love for others, regardless of how they respond to us.

SUMMARY

People can love and accept us only if they know who we really are, but fear of rejection prevents us from revealing our true selves. The fear of rejection is based on four assumptions, which all turn out to be myths.

Myth Number One: People Notice You. The reality is that no one is noticing you. People are too busy wondering about who might be noticing them to worry about noticing you. The fear of rejection begins with this key distraction: we spend too much energy wondering what others think about us.

Myth Number Two: You Can Know What Others Think. The reality is that you will never know for sure what others think about you. There are many reasons that someone, even someone you love, might not share with you their true perceptions.

Myth Number Three: We Can Control the Feelings of Others. The most destructive myth of all is that we can do things that will determine the feelings that others have for us. No matter what we do, the perceptions of others will always be beyond our control.

Myth Number Four: Perfection Attracts. Based on our observations of pop culture heroes, we have come to believe that perfection leads to love and acceptance. But it is our weaknesses and common flaws (when shared openly) that create bonds of love between us. Our strengths and apparent perfections may actually push us apart.

The ultimate fuel on which fear of rejection feeds is the preoccupation with ourself. We put too much time, energy, and anxiety into trying to influence what others think of us. The key to overcoming the fear of rejection is to focus our attention on expressing interest in and accepting others, rather than drowning in a sea of concern about whether or not others are going to accept us.

The Savior's sense of love and acceptance was based on what he felt for others and on his life of service to them. He did not waste his life trying to please others by conforming to their expectations. We must learn to judge ourselves more benevolently by looking at our hearts through the eyes of love. We must also focus our attention on the hearts of others through the same eyes of love. If we will do so, then we can overcome the fear of rejection.

CHAPTER SIX

HOW DO I LOVE THEE?

True Christianity is love in action.
—David O. McKay

Maslow argued that our need for love and acceptance could only be met externally through the loving expressions and actions of others. Ideally, he felt that this need would be met in childhood through positive interactions with parents and family members. But I have consistently observed that for those attending my classes, having been raised in a loving family is not enough. As college students and adults, the primary struggle for many, at least in Maslowian terms, is still to meet the need for love and acceptance. This is consistent with Dr. Dobson's finding that loneliness and lack of romance are among the leading causes of depression and unhappiness among women. It is also consistent with Maslow's belief that 98 percent of the population does not become self-actualized because of unmet needs for love, acceptance, and self-esteem.

But I can't help thinking, what if no one ever expresses love for you as an adult? Do you spend the rest of your life frustrated and unable to progress due to this unmet need? How do you get people to like you? If you can't get anyone to like you, then is it your fault if you never progress up the hierarchy to develop self-esteem or become self-actualized?

In chapter four we discounted the value of trying to create a façade so alluring that it can spontaneously invoke passion from others. But what's the alternative? What else are you going to do to get people to like you?

As discussed in chapter five, an important step in the right direction is to overcome the fear of rejection. By being open and authentic in our relations with others, we at least give them an opportunity to like the person that we really are (rather than a phony façade). But that still doesn't guarantee that anyone will care for us. What next?

Two Visions of Love

It seems that we may have been looking for love in all the wrong places. In the last chapter we learned that most people will never take much notice of us. Even if they did notice us, we will never know for sure what their perception was. And in any case, we cannot control what their perception will be. We concluded that we cannot depend on other people to fulfill our need for love and acceptance. Love and approval from others can be given and it can be taken away. If we look to others to meet our need for love, we may spend the rest of our lives stuck in the center of Maslow's hierarchy, unable to move up the pyramid. And so, rather than look for love in the eyes of others, perhaps we should be using our eyes to express it to them.

In short, I have at last come to the conclusion that whether or not we are able to meet the need for love and acceptance depends on our understanding of love and how we think it is obtained. First of all, then, we must come to an understanding of what love is.

Peas and Carrots

In order to demonstrate two different definitions of love, I turn to the innocent genius of Forrest Gump. I play the part of Forrest, while Brittany, the prom queen (who daily wonders when the class is going to get to the part about how we can lose weight), plays the part of Jenny. We pick up the story at the point that Jenny is being mocked and taunted by rowdies at the local bar.

On cue, the class starts throwing wadded up paper at Jenny and booing her. At last Forrest's simple devotion to Jenny is provoked to the point that it compels him to action. I sweep her up and carry her kicking and fighting to safety (the front of the classroom). After she is carefully set down, Jenny speaks angrily to me.

"Forrest," she says with exasperation, "why are you always rescuing me?"

This seems too obvious to require an explanation, but I slowly explain it to her anyway, answering with confused affection: "Because, I love you, Jenny."

"Forrest," she says with evident disgust, "you don't know what love is."

Forrest's defining characteristic is that he is slow. With this final insult to his intelligence, Jenny turns on her heel, catches a ride with a passing truck, and departs from Forrest's life for many years. Forrest is left standing on the sidewalk, confused but still devoted to Jenny. He takes every opportunity during the intervening years to express his love and concern for her by writing letters, but the only response he receives is a packet of his letters, returned, unopened.

Finally, after long years of drugs, promiscuity, and disappointments in love, Jenny runs out of options and returns to Alabama. She stays with Forrest while she tries to recover from her past. Brittany and I pick up the story in Forrest's living room at the point where Jenny is teaching Forrest how to dance. They have found their old friendship. As Forrest explains, he and Jenny are like "peas and carrots." As the dance concludes and Jenny prepares to retire for the evening, Forrest tentatively says, "Jenny, will you marry me? I'd make a good husband."

"Yes," Jenny answers guardedly, "you would make a good husband, Forrest." (Pause.)

"But you won't marry me." This time Forrest has the last word. "I am not a smart man," he says, "but I know what love is." (He turns and leaves.)

After a few moments of reflection, the class discusses the case of Forrest and Jenny. We try to analyze how each of them understood the concept of love and how they tried to meet their Maslowian needs for love and acceptance. "How does the understanding of love differ for Forrest and Jenny?" I ask.

TWO UNDERSTANDINGS OF LOVE

"For Jenny," Sarah offers after a few moments, "love is all about how *she* feels. It's the attention and praise she gets from others and the gratification that comes from those things. She tries to get it from the audiences she sings to or from her loser boyfriends, but in the end they all let her down and abandon her. The feelings of love are fleeting and insecure."

"For Forrest," Kristen says, "love is undying devotion and commitment to the welfare of *another* person, no matter how she treats him or what she does with her life. His love," she concludes shyly, "is constant and unfaltering."

"And so there are two different understandings of love," I offer. "For one it is a fleeting feeling that depends on the inconsistent, external actions and expressions of others. For the other, it is a constant sense of devotion that depends on an internal, personal commitment. And given these two understandings of love, who was most successful in meeting the need for love and acceptance?"

TWO APPROACHES FOR MEETING THE NEED FOR LOVE

There is silence in the room for some time before Carol attempts to answer the question. "Even though Jenny may have experienced occasions when audiences or boyfriends expressed love or appreciation for her, she ultimately failed to meet her need for love and acceptance. She came home broken and alone. I believe that she failed because of her reliance on others to make her feel good about herself. And those that she chose to associate with didn't really care about her. To them she was just a pretty toy—to be used and then tossed aside."

"Forrest, on the other hand," Sarah adds, "never worried about what others thought of him. He had no façades or false pretenses. He wasn't worried about being rejected by others. He had a deep devotion to someone else, and his concern was for her happiness. And somehow, even though love and acceptance wasn't expressed to him by others, he met his need for love and acceptance by feeling and expressing it for someone else."

LOOKING THROUGH THE EYES OF LOVE

While we do not have control over how others perceive us, we do have control over how we perceive them. We decide how much of our attention we devote to wondering if others favor us, and we decide how much of our attention we devote to seeing the hearts of others through the eyes of love. We decide if we love and accept them, and we determine through personal commitment to what extent we will express our love for them. It is my conviction that as adults our need for love and acceptance is not met externally through the loving expressions and actions of others (as theorized by Maslow). Instead, it is met as we develop feelings of love for others and then express that love to them in the form of a devoted commitment to their welfare and happiness.

And so the first step in meeting the need for love and acceptance is to forego creating façades and to rise above the fear of rejection to interact with others on the basis of our authentic self. Our authentic self means our weaknesses, vulnerabilities, and all. The second step is to turn our gaze outward. Instead of being preoccupied with trying to understand and control how others perceive us, we focus our attention on how we perceive them. We observe them closely and come to know the traits that make them unique and valuable—just as Forrest did with Jenny. As we do so, we learn to love others. If we will openly express our love and appreciation for them based on our perceptions of them, then our Maslowian need for love and acceptance will finally be met, and we can move on to higher concerns. Love is not an elusive reward that must be obtained externally from others by gaining the right appearance or the right characteristics. Instead, it is an ally that is standing ready within us to help us make peace with the image in the mirror.

Forrest had no fear of rejection because he wasn't worried about himself or how he was being perceived; he was worried about someone else. The reason that we fear rejection is that we feel that if it occurs it signifies that our need for love and acceptance cannot be met. But if our need for love and acceptance is met internally through our own determination to understand and love others, then rejection by others holds no power to deprive us of that need. Like Forrest, we extend our love to others and thereby meet our need for love and acceptance. Whether others accept or reject the love that we offer has greater implications for them than for us.

RECEIVING AND GIVING LOVE

These points are further emphasized through a thought experiment. I ask the students to close their eyes and think of a time when someone expressed unconditional love and acceptance for them. I watch them as they concentrate. Brittany has a wince on her face. Sarah carries a look of deep concern. Carol's face is lit up with a deep sense of satisfaction, and Kristen's face is crimson red. I give them several moments to think about this experience, and then I ask them to write down the feelings that occurred when unconditional love and acceptance was expressed for them.

"What types of feelings did you write down?" I ask.

"I thought of my three-year-old son," Carol explains. "Last night when I tucked him in, he gave me a big hug and said, 'Mommy, I love you.'" Tears are in her eyes as she says, "I wrote down the word *grateful*."

As other experiences are shared, we develop a list of positive feelings that includes gratitude, happiness, acceptance, safety, warmth, and a sense of being cared for. But then Sarah raises her hand and says quietly, "Dr. Hawks, I wasn't able to think of a time when another person expressed love and acceptance for me."

An uncomfortable silence fills the classroom until Brittany speaks up. "I had a really hard time with this too. But then I finally thought of an experience. But the feeling that went along with it was negative. It felt like a burden, or an obligation that I didn't want. I felt trapped and wanted to run away." (*Just like I ran away from Monica in first grade*, I think to myself. Even if other people love you, it may not do you any good.)

Kristen says, "For me the feeling was a sense of unworthiness. Sometimes I feel like if my fiancé knew what I was really like, he wouldn't be able to love me. I felt guilty."

To continue the experiment, I then ask the students to remember a time when they expressed unconditional love and acceptance for someone else. Every face has a smile as the students close their eyes and focus on their memories. After I ask them to write down the feelings that went along with these experiences, they are ready to comment.

Interestingly, all of the positive feelings on the previous list are repeated but none of the negative ones. Additionally, there are some new feelings.

"I felt noble," explains Carol. "I felt like I was rising above my own selfishness in an act that was truly noble."

"I felt like I was a genuinely good and kind person," Sarah says as she shares an experience about befriending an elementary schoolmate who was lonely.

In the end the two lists looked like this:

Receiving Love		Expressing Love	
Positive	Gratitude Happiness Acceptance Warmth/Safety Cared For	Gratitude Happiness Acceptance Warmth/Safety Cared For	*Positive*
Negative	Obligated Guilty Unworthy	Noble Selfless Kind and Good	*Empowered*

The Maslowian need for love and acceptance, when met, is characterized by feelings of gratitude, happiness, acceptance, warmth, and a sense of being cared for. If we try to obtain these feelings by prying expressions of love from others, then success will be uncertain at best.

Fortunately, we are in control of how we feel about others and how we express our feelings toward them. If we *express* our love for them through a lifetime of commitment to their welfare, we will experience all the positive feelings that are associated with *receiving* love. In addition, we will experience inner growth and development as we rise above the preoccupation with self. President Hinckley explained that "the real essence of happiness in marriage lies not so much in romance as in an anxious concern for the comfort and well-being of one's companion."[1] Forrest was right on track.

THE GREEK CONCEPT OF LOVE

It is interesting to consider the above concepts in light of three classical Greek terms for the concept of love: *eros*, *filos*, and *agapê*. Eros constitutes physical intimacy and is most often used in the context of sexual relations. *Filos*, on the other hand, represents fondness or affection. Regardless of the gender involved, *filos* implies feelings of brotherly affection for others. Finally, *agapê* connotates a conscious decision to express loving commitment for others as guided by spiritual ideals. It represents self-denying and compassionate devotion.

While Forrest may have had aspirations for erotic love and while he may have had genuine feelings of brotherly affection for Jenny (filos), he was able to express self-denying devotion and commitment for Jenny's welfare (agapê) even if the other forms of love were not present or were even rejected. Jenny, on the other hand, was convinced that eros was the true and singular definition of love, and she pursued it until she was spent and broken. She may have had brotherly affection, or filos, in relation to Forrest, but it did not develop into agapê until after the other forms of love had failed to meet her real needs and she was finally softened by the devotion of Forrest.

While we all have strong desires in relation to all three types of love, it is the development and expression of agapê that allows us to meet the Maslowian need for love and acceptance. If our fellow creatures never deem us fit to be the recipients of brotherly love and affection (filos) and if we never find the romance that we dream about (eros), we can still meet our need for love and acceptance by embracing the spiritual imperative to love one another. Fortunately, as we follow that path we also increase our chances of becoming part of a circle of brotherly love and of finding a soul mate with whom we might appropriately develop a passionate romance.

SPIRITUAL SOLUTIONS

Before we can truly love others in the form of agapê, however, we must have a spiritual source of inspiration. That inspiration can be found in the belief that each person is a child of God who possesses unique spiritual gifts. As spiritual brothers and sisters, we have the opportunity to help each other open and share those gifts for our mutual enjoyment. As taught by the apostle Paul, "the manifestation of the Spirit is given to every man to profit withal" (1 Corinthians 12:7). This foundation for love is discussed further in chapter nine.

"Sarah," I try to explain by way of conclusion, "just because you can't think of a time when someone expressed love for you doesn't mean that no one has ever felt love for you. Within this room I don't think that I'm alone in my feelings of admiration, respect, and love for the person that you are (filos). But even more important than what others feel for you is the unique ability that you have to feel and express love for others (agapê)—just like you did for your classmate back in elementary school."

The Savior never taught that we should seek to be loved by others. Instead, he said, "A new commandment I give unto you, That ye love one another; as I have loved you, that ye also love one another" (John 13:34).

Expressing unconditional love and acceptance for others will not protect us from the inevitable disappointments and frustrations that we all experience in courtship and romance, marital relationships, and relationships with our parents or children. But it will enable us to move upward and onward with our lives and free us from the destructive pastime of trying to inspire love in others by attempting to be irresistibly wonderful. As we proceed along such a course, the power of the mirror continues to fade.

SUMMARY

According to Maslow, the need for love and acceptance is met in childhood by loving parents and families. But many adults continue to struggle with this need, even if they came from a loving family.

The first step in meeting this need for love and acceptance is to rise above the fear of rejection by living an authentic life that encourages the discovery of the true self and that allows people to know and accept you for who you really are.

In order to take the second step, we must come to an understanding of what love means to us. For many, like Jenny, love is the feeling that is experienced in response to external expressions of love or admiration. But this form of love is fleeting, uncontrollable, unpredictable, and undependable. For Forrest, love is a conscious decision to remain devoted to the welfare of another person, regardless of how that person responds. This type of love is within our control: it is dependable, predictable, and lasting. Ultimately, it is the source of happiness in all of our relationships. In Greek terminology, it is called *agapê*.

If others express love for us, which may or may not happen, the experience will generally be positive, but it can also cause discomfort, negative feelings, and guilt. When we express love for others, it is almost always a positive experience that has all the characteristics of receiving love but also ennobles and uplifts us as we rise above our selfish interests. It is the only sure way to experience all the positive and empowering feelings associated with Maslow's concept of love and acceptance. The Maslowian need for love and acceptance is primarily met as we express love for others, not as we receive it from them.

Frustrations and disappointments in love are an inevitable part of this life. It took many years before Jenny responded to Forrest's love for her. Some never respond, not even to the Savior's love. But our ability to meet the need for love and acceptance, and then move on to higher Maslowian needs, cannot be denied to us if we will open our hearts and focus our attention on expressing love to others—no matter how they respond. The inspiration that gives rise to our love for others can be found in the belief that each person is a child of God possessing unique spiritual gifts. This belief is not only central to meeting our need for love and acceptance, but it is central to the concept of self-esteem—the topic of the next section.

SECTION III

THE PATH TO SELF-ESTEEM

Another compelling reason that we concern ourselves with our reflected image is because of the influence that we allow it to exert on our sense of self-worth, or self-esteem. Too often, we use our unacceptable appearance as a scapegoat on which to blame our failures and lack of a committed, passionate life. In a downward spiral, many of our perceived inadequacies become intertwined and mingled with, perhaps even inseparable from, our dissatisfaction with our appearance. Our attention is thereby distracted from where it might best be focused, and the image in the mirror takes up an excessive amount of time, energy, and other resources, while meaningful self-development stagnates.

In order to break away from this cycle, it is important to evaluate different definitions of the concept of self-esteem and to come to an understanding about how true self-esteem is fostered. This is the goal of Section three.

CHAPTER SEVEN

SELF-ESTEEM AS VANITY

In my day we didn't have self-esteem, we had self-respect,
and no more of it than we had earned.
—Jane Haddam

As adults, our need for love and acceptance is met as we do three things: (a) learn to live an authentic life (free of façades), (b) surrender the preoccupation with ourself in favor of a genuine interest in others, and (c) express our love openly and unconditionally by making a conscious commitment to be concerned with the welfare and happiness of all those within our reach. Once this orientation is firmly rooted in our character, then we can stand upon that foundation and concern ourselves with the higher concept of self-esteem. As in a canal system, where locks are filled with water, a lock of love will be filled, lifting us up and allowing us to sail into the new, but as yet unfilled lock of self-esteem. How will we fill up this new lock?

The answer, or at least a clue, comes from Henry David Thoreau, the great philosopher who wrote of the insights he gained while living a passionate but simple life on the banks of Walden Pond. Equipped with a stout walking stick, dressed in the plain attire of early America, and adorned with wire-rimmed spectacles, I approach my students and use Thoreau's words to address them in earnest:

"I went to the woods because I wished to live deliberately, to front only the essential facts of life, and see if I could not learn what it had to teach, and not, when I came to die, discover that I had not lived. I did not wish to live what was not life, living is so dear, nor did I wish to practice resignation, unless it was quite necessary. I wanted to live deep and suck out all the marrow of life, to live so sturdily and Spartan-like as to put to rout all that was not life, to cut a broad swath and shave close, to drive life into a corner, and reduce it to its lowest terms, and, if it proved to be mean, why then to get the whole mean-ness of it, and publish its meanness to the world; or if it were sublime, to know it by experience, and be able to give a true account of it in my next excursion."[1]

"Even though some of his meanings may not be readily per-ceived," I say while waving the walking stick dramatically, "Henry David Thoreau has given us a master plan for fulfilling the human need that Maslow labeled 'self-esteem.' Before we can fully grasp all the subtle doctrines contained in his message, we must lay a foun-dation."

As a class we begin by attempting to grasp the true importance of self-esteem by making a list of social problems to which low self-esteem (it is popularly believed) may contribute. Before long our list becomes quite long and includes gang involvement, drug experi-mentation, violence, promiscuity, juvenile delinquency, eating disorders, divorce, drug addiction, obsession with thinness, alco-holism, unstable relationships, poor school performance, lack of happiness and fulfillment in life, and so on. If the research literature that ties low self-esteem to these social problems is accurate, then finding ways to enhance self-esteem among the members of our soci-ety would seem to be of the utmost importance to all of us.[2]

Defining Self-Esteem

"But what is a good definition of self-esteem?" I ask. "What is it exactly that we are trying to improve?" After some debate, the class agrees that self-esteem should be defined broadly as "a personal assess-ment of the worth of the self."

We are led to believe that many of our most pressing social problems arise, at least in part, because there are many who *assess the value of their self* as being low. In a misguided way, some people attempt to deal with the pain of believing that their worth is low by engaging in behaviors that allow them to escape from the pain, or at least to dull it. Hence the relationship develops between low self-esteem and eating disorders, promiscuity, drug abuse, and other mind-altering and addictive behaviors that help take us away from the disappointment of reality.

But by taking a more positive approach, others deal with feelings of low self-esteem by engaging in behaviors that they hope will change the worth of the self and hence their assessment of it. And in fact, isn't the goal of the modern "self-esteem movement" to help us find ways to increase the value that we place on ourselves?

If we would reduce the social problems associated with low self-esteem, then the goal of society should be to help those who have low self-esteem find positive ways to change their assessment of self-worth without resorting to the negative or harmful behaviors that we listed on the chalkboard. But we must make sure that our underlying assumptions are accurate or the result may not be what was intended.

SOCIETY'S SOLUTION FOR SELF-ESTEEM

Perhaps the best way to understand modern, social approaches for enhancing self-esteem is to take an example. Because of all the social and academic problems experienced by adolescents in relation to self-esteem, school districts have attempted to tackle this issue.

"Let's begin by analyzing the public education system to gain insight into one approach that society uses to enhance the self-esteem of young people," I offer at the beginning of class. "And then we can ask ourselves if the methods employed by society, as manifested by the education system, can be successful in raising self-esteem and promoting the happiness and well-being of the individual."

Several education majors look threatened by the implication that I may be preparing to cast an unfavorable light on the profession they intend to join. Their eyes reveal the same distrust that might exist if they knew I was about to try to persuade them that apple pie should no longer be considered American. My grip instinctively tightens about my walking stick.

"How do teachers try to enhance the self-esteem of their students?" I ask innocently. The education majors are not slow to offer examples.

"By creating opportunities for each student to achieve success," says one.

"By praising them at every opportunity," says another.

"By giving them lots of awards and recognition," says a third.

The Fallacy of External Rewards

"Achievement, success, praise, and recognition feel good don't they?" I say supportively. "Kind of like eating chocolate feels good." Suddenly the eyes of one of the students narrow menacingly as she smells the trap. Before she can rally her colleagues for a counter-offensive, I try to gain support from the rest of the class by asking, "Is there a danger in basing assessments of personal worth on such outcomes as success, praise, and recognition?"

Sarah raises her hand and offers support for my position. "It teaches them that to feel good about themselves they must obtain some form of external reward. The worth of the self is measured by the teacher's ruler. They learn that in order to feel good about themselves, they must compete with each other by trying to be the best at jumping through the hoops that the teacher holds up for them."

"The message is that to judge your own worth, you should rely on a wink or a nod from society," adds Carol. "If the winks and nods don't come, then you are conditioned to think of yourself as a failure. In that case personal assessments of self-worth may decline. If the winks and nods do come, you may become addicted to them as a way to feel good about yourself—just like some people become addicted to the pleasure of chocolate as a way to feel good."

Kristen adds a comment: "Students become too preoccupied with trying to conform and live up to narrow measures of educational success. They are never given the opportunity to look inside and discover their own standards and values."

Narcissism

"Take the case of my ten-year-old son, Jeremiah," I offer by way of example. "We had been invited to the principal's office on more than one occasion to discuss Jeremiah's behavior problems. Imagine our surprise when one day he comes home and shows us a very nice certificate identifying him as the student of the month for his elementary school. Our eyes filled with tears. We knelt and gave him a big hug and rejoiced at this sign that he had overcome his challenges and risen to the top of his class. But then Jeremiah took the certificate, wadded it up, and threw it away. 'Every kid gets one of these, Dad,' he explained with a disgusted 'humph.' 'They don't mean anything.'

"When we commence to manufacture false awards under the pretense of making someone feel that their worth has gone up, then we engage in flattery and do them a disservice," I explain. "On the one hand they become conditioned to believe that their individual value is determined externally by others and is only of genuine worth when validated by a certificate. This approach may impair the person's ability to eventually recognize their worth from an internal perspective in the absence of external rewards.

"On the other hand, spurious awards and recognition may create a false sense of ego gratification that leads to narcissism, an exaggerated sense of self-importance that has no basis in actual achievement or development. When the fragile ego is challenged, the result can be violence. The person lashes out to defend personal worth that has no other means of validation. Some research indicates that this sense of narcissism is a factor in many of the school shootings that plague the nation.[3] If Jeremiah had taken his certificate and paraded around the school touting his importance, for example, sooner or later someone would have pointed out that he was still the same old Jeremiah, with or without the certificate. If he had placed great stock in the certificate as an indicator of his worth and importance, the result would have been anger and maybe even a fight."

Defensive is not a strong enough word to describe the state of mind at which the education majors have now arrived. Trying to ward off a coordinated attack, I sally into their midst while brandishing my walking stick.

"I believe with all my heart," I say passionately to the education students, "that teachers in this country care very deeply about their students and do everything they can to enhance their well-being. In order to make my point, I have been simplistic and overly broad in my generalizations. I apologize. After all, I am also a member of the profession.

"At the same time," I acknowledge with equal emotion, "I believe that in some cases those within the school system become the unwitting supporters of larger social forces that actually undermine the development of true self-esteem."

Fallacies Exposed

While the peace is a tentative one, it lasts long enough for me to ascend my soap box and make a final assessment. "First of all," I begin, "the educational system defines 'normal' too narrowly and recognizes and rewards only those who do well in a left-brained, materialistic society. We define the rest as being disordered and place them on Ritalin." Two students have to hold back Kristen, the nurse, who looks as if she would like to take my stick and smack me with it.

"Secondly," I continue, "the school system fails to appreciate and support the full range of human potential. It rewards only those that correlate with things praised by society (for example, beauty, talent, academic intelligence) but discounts all others. The internal, spiritual attributes of inner genius such as caring, warmth of personality, creativity, enthusiasm, kindness, imagination, leadership, and physical energy are at best ignored and at worst medicated." Kristen looks like she's going to explode. At great peril I continue to ignore her.

"Finally," I say, while adjusting my Thoreauian spectacles and assuming the stance of a great statesman, "the educational system helps create a colony of obedient ants that evaluate normalcy and personal worth in terms of their ability to follow along behind all the other ants. However," I emphasize, just before the education majors let Kristen go, "education is not the real problem. The educational system is simply one expression of a social tradition whose faulty assumptions are seldom challenged."

THE VALUE-ADDED PARADIGM OF SELF-ESTEEM

This concession buys me an additional moment in which to continue my crusade. "In the case of society at large and the educational system in particular," I argue, "the underlying assumption in relation to self-esteem is a damning one. Central to our social concept of self-esteem, as defined and discussed above, is the belief that self-esteem is enhanced when our personal assessment of worth changes. If our assessment of worth can change," I argue, "then our assumption must be that the actual worth of the self can also change. As such, we might call this the *value-added paradigm of self-esteem* (that is, our assessment of personal worth is enhanced as we accomplish things that add value to that worth)."

Like a Potato Chip

"In the value-added paradigm, we try to enhance self-esteem by altering the worth of the self and hence our assessment of that worth.

(Just like Clover Club adds value to a potato by slicing it, adding salt, and deep frying it.) As defined by society, which is the only standard we are taught to judge by, the worth of an individual is measured externally in terms of those things that society extols—appearance, social status, wealth, possessions, fame, talent, etc. We are led to believe that if we obtain those things, our personal worth will change accordingly. The educational system innocently supports this line of reasoning by trying to promote self-esteem through the external avenues of success, recognition, and praise."

"Other forces in society," I add, "also encourage this paradigm of self-esteem because their purposes are best served if they can turn us into paranoid, materialistic consumers who think we can add to our personal value through the purchase of inherently worthless aids, such as beauty, health, fitness, and other commercial products. Our self-esteem is like a raw potato. Society tells us that if we will change in certain dictated ways (get sliced thinly, dosed with salt, and fried in fat), then we can be transformed into a much more valuable person. And so we get in line to jump in the fire. This is good for those who profit from the manufacture of potato chips, but it's not necessarily good for the potato. Likewise, our attempts to add value to our self in socially defined ways may serve the interests of those who profit from our efforts, but it does little for our own growth and development.

"For example," I offer, "what happens to the self-esteem of most females in this country when they arrive at adolescence?"

As if speaking from experience, Brittany, the prom queen, says, "It drops like a stone in a pond."

"Why?" I probe.

"Because the worth of the self suddenly comes to be judged almost solely on the criteria of appearance," she says with emotion, "and the external standard of appearance that has been established by this society is so unreasonable that almost no one can live up to it.[4] In light of our discussion," she adds with a sad smile, "maybe it should be called the value-subtracted paradigm. There are far more things that tear our worth down than that build it up."

A Misguided Paradigm

"As our society continues to support the value-added (or value-subtracted) paradigm of self-esteem," I say as I point to the chalkboard, "what will be the likely impact on our list of social problems?"

"If anything," Carol notes, "it is likely to increase pleasure seeking and mindless attempts at social conformity as we try to jump through the hoops that will supposedly make us more worthwhile. There will probably be even more addiction, obsession, frustration, despair, boredom, and lack of satisfaction with life. Crime, violence, deviant behavior, and addictions will probably continue to increase as we try to escape the pain that accompanies our failure to toe the line that society has created for us."

After agreeing with Carol's assessment, I conclude that the value-added paradigm represents a misguided approach for understanding and promoting self-esteem. Rather than true self-esteem, it promotes the pursuit of vanity and results in frustrated egotism. Hence the ability of this philosophy to relieve social problems is minimal at best, and it may even actively contribute to some of the social ills mentioned by Carol. But worst of all, the value-added paradigm decoys us away from the real path that leads to self-esteem.

WHEN I LOOK GOOD, I FEEL BETTER ABOUT MYSELF

To wrap up our discussion, I ask the students, "How many of you agree with the statement 'When I look good, I feel better about myself'?" It never fails to surprise me that in spite of our discussion to this point, almost all hands go up.

"Identify a word," I challenge, "that most fully describes the value-added paradigm of self-esteem." After numerous attempts, no one comes up with the word I am after. I give them a decisive hint. "The value-added paradigm," I explain, "is characterized by three things: (a) an arbitrary, external standard or measure of acceptability, (b) a comparison of the self against that standard (and against others who are competing against the same standard), and (c) the belief that worth changes, in relation to the former self and in relation to others, as one comes closer to meeting the standard of acceptability."

As several more guesses fail to reveal the sought-after word, I am reluctantly forced to supply it myself (even though I realize that to do so will place me in some danger). "It starts with a 'V,'" I explain, "and rhymes with *sanity*." Still there is no answer.

"*Vanity*," I shout in spite of the glares, "pure and simple vanity. Trying to add value to the worth of the self through external accomplishments (and comparison to others) is called vanity. We are vain when we think that our worth has changed in relation to our former self or to others simply because we have been successful in measuring up to an external yardstick." I note with concern that all students seem to have joined forces with the education majors.

"The phrase 'when I look good' implies an external standard that defines what 'good-looking' means. Without an external standard, there is no basis for subjective comparison, and the phrase loses all meaning. The phrase 'I feel better about myself' implies that one's personal assessment of self-worth has changed as a function of coming closer to the external standard for looking good." The united students seem to be making plans together. It looks as if Kristen has been designated as their leader.

"And so to say, 'When I look good, I feel better about myself,'" I continue, "really means, 'When I am successful in conforming to external standards of beauty, I derive pleasure from gratifying my vanity.'" My small walking stick will afford scant protection, I think to myself, as a mutinous murmur swells through the classroom. I conclude that a riot is imminent and decide to strike a final blow before the crowd erupts.

"*Now* how many of you would agree," I roar above the din, "that 'When I look good, I feel better about myself'?" Rather than exemplify the spirit of Thoreau by trying to "cut a broad swath and drive life into a corner," I quickly announce a ten-minute break and sprint for the safety of my office. A more complete discussion of Thoreau's ideas and virtues will have to wait for the next session of class.

SPIRITUAL SOLUTIONS

The words *look good* in the phrase, "When I *look good*, I feel better about myself," could be replaced by several other terms without losing any meaning. "When I [own a sports car] [have lots of money] [achieve fame] [win the lottery] [am the expert] [have power], I feel better about myself." All of these phrases can represent a false sense of heightened personal worth when they really amount to nothing more than the pride of social achievement. The "I feel better about myself" part of the phrase represents the gratification of vanity, not an increase in the value of the self. As revealed in the Book of Mormon, we must be wary of relying on such conditions to feel better about ourselves.

On the positive side, it is interesting that during a righteous period the Nephites "did not wear costly apparel, yet they were neat and comely" (Alma 1:27). Rather than saying "when I *look good*," perhaps we should say, "when I am *neat and comely*, then I feel better about myself." The latter implies a concern for hygiene and modesty, while the former connotes a reliance on being fashionable in order to feel acceptable.

During the final fall of the Nephites, it is significant that in the very first verse in which Mormon chronicles the emerging change from righteousness to wickedness, he says, "There began to be among them those who were lifted up in pride, such as the wearing of costly apparel, and all manner of fine pearls, and of the fine things of the world" (4 Nephi 1:24). From there things get worse until "there never had been so great wickedness among all the children of Lehi" (Mormon 4:12). And it all began with the pride that comes from trying to "look good to feel better."

SUMMARY

The modern concept of self-esteem can generally be defined as "a personal assessment of the value of the self." According to this definition, those who assess their personal worth as low will experience pain that may be relieved in negative ways. Hence, low self-esteem is thought to be a causal factor underlying many social ills. In an attempt to alleviate these ills, some institutions attempt to increase positive assessments of personal worth by creating narrowly defined opportunities for external success, praise, and recognition.

"Adding value" to the self through external rewards will presumably result in higher self-evaluations of worth. But the approach is based on false principles: (a) narrow and arbitrary standards of acceptability, (b) comparisons of the self against the standards, and (c) the belief that worth changes as standards are achieved. It has been taken to the point that many certificates of achievement are not based on true excellence but are instead shallow attempts to invoke feelings of esteem without merit. You are allowed to "measure up" without having to achieve.

At best, the result is the mere gratification of vanity. In the meantime, the ability to appreciate our unique inner value is lost, and we become dependent on recognition doled out by others in order to define our worth. At worst, attempts to bolster self-esteem that rely on meaningless external recognition may predispose some individuals to be aggressive and violent if their ungrounded sense of self-importance is challenged.

This value-added definition and approach to self-esteem not only fails to redress the social ills of our day, it may actively contribute to them. In conclusion, attempts to add value to the self in socially defined ways may serve the interests of others, but it does little for personal growth and development.

CHAPTER EIGHT

SELF-ESTEEM AS JOY

Trust yourself, then you will know how to live.
—Johann Wolfgang von Goethe

At the beginning of the next class session, I try to make amends for the quarrelsome ending detailed in the last chapter by sharing with the students my reflections on a personal weakness. "My approach to pursuing my doctoral degree," I begin, "is a good example of the value-added approach to self-esteem. I pursued the degree largely with the expectation that I would be more worthwhile when I had increased my personal value by measuring up to the yardstick of academic merit. Once the degree was earned, I believed, I would somehow be better because I could append the letters 'Ed.D.' to my name. It was pure and simple vanity," I sigh.

"As far as helping me recognize the value of my potential and make strides toward realizing it, my education was not put to good purpose. Instead of an opportunity for learning, my list of required courses served as a mere checklist with which to tick off each rung of the ladder that led to the coveted diploma. As a result, I didn't learn much." I then share this poem with the class:

> There was an old man from Esser,
> Whose knowledge grew lesser and lesser,
> It at last grew so small, he knew nothing at all,
> And now he's a college professor.

How ironic to finally get the resplendent diploma only to realize as I entered my first classroom as a "college professor" that I epitomized the old man from Esser—virtual ignorance. Almost all of my growth and development as an individual happened after I earned my degree and realized that being a good college professor was not a magical gift that was conferred with a diploma. Instead, I found, it was a lifelong process that required diligent study, effort, and experience. My biggest regret is that I could have gotten a much better start if I would have approached my coursework as a valuable learning process rather than as a stairway to personal glory.

I think back to the words of Thoreau as presented at the beginning of chapter seven and try to imagine a better way. Thoreau's approach was to "live deep and suck out all the marrow of life, to live so sturdily and Spartan-like as to put to rout all that was not life."[1] It is all about gaining knowledge and wisdom through diligent experience and study. There is nothing about gaining prestige. If only we could apply Thoreau's attitude toward life to the process of learning, we might say something like this:

"I went to school because I wished to learn deliberately, to front only the essential facts, and see if I could not grasp what they had to teach, and not, when I came to graduate, discover that I had not learned."

It seems important to be preoccupied with a passion to understand and discover ourselves and our world and "know them by experience," rather than be preoccupied with trying to ascend a pedestal so that we can be admired by others. The former leads to inner growth and development, while the latter descends into vanity and conceited posturing.

It is said of Sir Isaac Newton that he would become so involved with study and experiments that he would repeatedly forget to eat dinner. Those who were close to him feared that he might actually study himself to death. And yet that would perhaps be a better demise than one resulting from frustrated egotism. Newton did not go through the motions of learning so that he could jump through the academic hoops that would lead to a prestigious degree. Instead, he rolled up his sleeves and applied himself to his books and laboratories so that he could increase his understanding and then use that understanding to enlighten those around him.[2] The knowledge we obtain through study and experience blesses us and those around us, and then it rises with us in the next life. The flattery that fans our vanity blesses no one, and then it is left in the grave forever.

CONSIDERING THE ALTERNATIVE

The next point that requires elaboration as we try to understand self-esteem is presented to the class in the form of a question. "What is the alternative," I ask, "to believing that the worth of the self changes as a function of our accomplishments, such as earning a college degree? What is the alternative to believing that we will be *better* if we can just measure up to the social yardsticks that have been established for beauty, knowledge, power, or wealth?"

"The alternative," Sarah explains matter-of-factly, "is to believe that the worth of the self does not change, even if you do earn a degree or win an Academy Award or attain some other high recognition."

"Exactly," I affirm. "But if we conclude that the worth of the self doesn't change, then what provides the self with worth in the first place? Or, of ourselves, do we have any worth at all?"

This is a difficult question, and at first no one attempts a response. Yet the answer to the dilemma of whether or not we have inherent, unalterable worth has more significance than the resolution of a parlor room debate. What we believe and how we behave in relation to the Maslowian need for realizing self-esteem is determined by how we deal with the question of inner worth. Does our personal value change with external achievement, or is our worth fixed and inherent?

As has already been discussed, the belief that self-worth changes in response to external accomplishment is characterized by trying to favorably alter the value of the self by seeking the praise, recognition, and rewards that society offers for narrowly defined achievements. At best we gratify vanity; at worst we waste our energy and lose opportunities for true development (as in the example of my college career).

On the other hand, where will we be led if we believe that the value of the self is precious, already inherent within us, and unchangeable—no matter what we do with it? It is a question worth exploring with the students in my class.

THE INHERENT-VALUE PARADIGM

"What would happen to our definition of self-esteem," I ask the class to ponder, "if we believed that the value of the self was eternal, inherent, and fixed, and nothing that we did, good or bad, could add to or subtract from that inherent worth?"

There is a thoughtful pause before Carol finally ventures an answer. "The entire concept of self-esteem would cease to have meaning," she begins, "at least in the way that we have defined it. We said that self-esteem was a personal assessment of the value of the self. If the value of the self doesn't change—no matter what we do—then personal assessments in relation to the worth of the self would have no purpose. By definition the assessment would always be the same and therefore pointless."

The Worth of the Self

"Very good," I reply. "But now we must go back to our original question: What would the unchangeable worth of the self be based on? Why would there be any worth in the first place?"

After thinking carefully for a moment, Carol continues by saying,

"Would it be because we are members of the human family and are thereby endowed with all the potential and possibilities that characterize the most noble aspects of human nature? We have inherent worth because we have the human ability to make a unique contribution."

"Yes! The value of the self is based on the reality that we have innate potential that exists within us by virtue of our belonging to the human race. The worth of that potential will not be diminished or increased by one iota, whether we develop our potential or allow it to go unrealized, because the worth of our potential arises from the fact that we *can* make a difference, not that we *do* make a difference."

Measuring Self-Worth

These are not easy concepts to explain or to grasp, but as a class we decide to forge ahead with more questioning that will hopefully shed light on this difficult subject. "How can we place a value on our potential?" I continue. "By what yardstick can we measure the relative worth of our potential?"

There is a long pause before Sarah hazards a guess. "If our potential is unique to us," she begins, "then it cannot be expressed in any other fashion than through its realization in our individual lives. And if it truly represents one possible expression of the highest aspirations of humankind, then the worth of our self is infinite, priceless, and incapable of being compared against the worth of other potentials. There is no way to place a value on the worth of the self (as embodied by our human potential) or to compare its value in relation to the value of others."

"Exactly," I concede. "The value of the self, as defined by our potential, is priceless, infinite, unique, and immeasurable. As such, there is no point in trying to make a personal assessment of the value of the self. The old definition of self-esteem is invalid, and so is the path to fulfillment that it recommends. But if the path to achieving self-esteem by jumping through artificial hoops, as suggested by the value-added paradigm, is not valid," I continue, "then what path must we follow if we want to develop true self-esteem?"

A New Path to Self-Esteem

The new path would have to begin with an understanding that we do indeed embody valuable potential. The purpose of life would then be to develop and express that potential. But if the value of the self won't change one way or the other by realizing or wasting inherent potential, then what will change if potential is in fact realized? In short, why should we want to realize our potential if it won't change our worth or add to our status among our fellow citizens?

First of all, if we had a correct understanding of our own potential, a tremendous burden would be taken away as we no longer felt the need to compete with each other in trying to prove our worth by measuring up to social yardsticks. Secondly, the burden that was lifted would be replaced with the delightful realization that we are already endowed with tremendous worth without a need to prove anything. Finally, we would be filled with the desire to try to understand our potential and develop it to the fullest degree possible.

The consequence would be the same passion that Newton felt for his work and the same intensity that Thoreau applied to his life. The primary reason for striving to recognize and realize our potential would be the joy we would experience as our capacity grew to the point that we were able to develop new insights and make a genuine contribution to the world around us.

A NEW DEFINITION FOR SELF-ESTEEM

Rather than define self-esteem as a personal assessment of the value of the self, we should perhaps define it as *a sense of joy that is experienced when inherent potential is discovered and realized.* The essence of this definition is captured in the words of the great philosopher Kierkegaard:

"If I were to wish for anything, I should not wish for wealth and power, but for the passionate sense of potential—for the eye which, ever young and ardent, sees the possible. Pleasure disappoints; possibility never."

As recognized by Kierkegaard, true joy comes from recognizing and then striving to realize inherent potential, not from trying to add value to the self through the accumulation of wealth or power or beauty. True self-esteem comes from the feeling that you possess the ability to make a difference. All that is required is the passion to execute the possibility.

Rather than waste our efforts on vainly trying to assess the value of our worth, which is constant and unchangeable, we should focus our attention on trying to experience joy through developing our potential and sharing it with others. This is the true meaning of self-esteem, and it is a very real need in Maslow's hierarchy. Without the foundation that this type of self-esteem can provide, we cannot consider the higher need of self-actualization.

We must remember the wisdom of the great knight Don Quixote as he exhorts himself to "*Love not what thou art, but only what thou may become.*" (That is, don't indulge in the vanity of speculating about your personal worth but be passionate about becoming who you are through the realization of personal potential.)

A comparison of the value-added and inherent-value paradigms of self-esteem is provided in the box on the next page. In the value-added column, false self-esteem is pursued with the assumption that our accomplishments change our relative worth. The focus is on self-comparison against social standards, and the result is either gratified vanity (if we compare favorably) or frustrated vanity (if the mirror tells us that we are not worthy). We are preoccupied with ourself, and we continually wonder how others perceive us.

Self-Esteem	
Value-Added (Personal Assessment of value of self)	**Inherent-Value** (Joy of sharing potential with others)
Value of self changes	Value of self is fixed and constant
Based on accomplishment	Based on inherent potential
Measured by external yardsticks	Realized by inner development
Relies on comparison	Celebrates uniqueness
Focus is on self	Focus is on others
The result is **Vanity**	*The result is* **Joy**

In the inherent-value approach, self-esteem is pursued with the assumption that we are already endowed with worth based on our human potential and that nothing we can do will alter the value of that worth. The focus is on discovering and realizing unique potential so that our capacity will develop to the point that we can make a meaningful contribution to the world around us. Like Thoreau and Newton, we will live life fully and passionately with little concern for personal prestige. The result is either the joy that comes from discovering and sharing our potential or the nagging frustration that plagues those who fail to understand who they really are and what they have to offer.

SELF-ESTEEM AND EDUCATION

"What are the implications of the inherent-value paradigm for education," I ask, "in terms of how we foster self-esteem among children?"

One of the education majors, flanked dangerously by the nurse Kristen, tentatively says, "We could encourage the joy of self-discovery and inner development, rather than rely on external praise and rewards to foster conformity. Also, we could be more tolerant of those with diverse potentials that do not directly reflect those things that society rewards."

"And we could allow for a broader range of normalcy with a wider variety of student-teacher interactions," Kristen adds reluctantly, "rather than prematurely resort to drugs to control behavior. Most important, we could provide opportunities for children to experience the joy of sharing their unique talents with each other as those talents are developed."

"Excellent comments," I reply sincerely, and Kristen even smiles at me. "Given limited budgets, low salaries, overcrowded classrooms, scarce resources, and many other limitations, it does not represent an easy task," I confess. "But I believe that major improvements are possible if enlightened educators apply themselves with conviction."

Research has shown that young children who are praised for a particular trait, being smart, for example, tend to experience more anxiety and higher rates of failure when faced with a task that requires the demonstration of that trait.[3] If we praise Johnny for being really good at math and then offer him a hard math problem, he will be afraid of that problem. Because if he fails to solve it he will lose identification with the one trait that seems to define his greatest value (and lose the praise that goes along with it). This is the fallacy of basing our self-worth on an identification with traits that can so easily fail us. The idea of having personal value that is based on having a desirable trait (such as intelligence or beauty) is part of the value-added paradigm of self-esteem. The approach breeds fear, anxiety, and failure. No wonder, then, that those who are praised for beauty are at increased risk for eating disorders.[4]

On the other hand, students who are praised for being hard workers (rather than for being smart) will view new, difficult tasks, such as a hard math problem, as an exciting challenge rather than a menacing threat. And because of their attitude, they are more likely to succeed at solving the problem regardless of their level of math intelligence. The idea of putting forth personal effort to realize inner development and overcome challenges is characteristic of the inherent-value paradigm of self-esteem. It breeds hard work and confidence and leads to success in turning difficult challenges into opportunities for self-discovery and personal growth.

Referring back to our original list of social problems, I ask the students, "What would be the impact on these problems if self-esteem were approached from the inherent-value paradigm?" Well-thought-out answers soon come.

"Relationships would be more giving and stable when people lost the need to compete with one another and recognized the larger value and joy of supporting each other's inner growth and development."

"Like Kierkegaard explained, children would be more excited about the possibility of realizing their potential and less interested in escaping through harmful pleasures like sex, drugs, and alcohol."

Self-Esteem and the Image in the Mirror

"In the value-added paradigm of self-esteem, what is the role of appearance?" I ask.

"Thinness, a pretty face, the right hair, a nice shape, and the achievement of other physical perfections become ways to try to add value to the self," Kristen comments. "As we begin to feel superior by measuring up to those yardsticks, our vanity is gratified. Our 'perfect' body or 'perfect' looks become an object of gratification for others and for ourselves. We use them to lift ourselves up and put others down. We become a golden potato chip to everyone else's unpeeled potato. But we can see all the other potatoes working really hard to become better chips than us, and so we are filled with relentless fear and anxiety that we may not always be the best chip. And in the end, beauty always fails; the fragile chip crumbles."

"At the same time," Carol adds, "the imperfect body or other flaws of appearance turn our image into the enemy and cause us deep resentment toward our bodies. We continually beat ourselves up for just being plain old potatoes. We pin our hopes on someday becoming attractive chips and in the meantime miss out on inner development and the realization of our true potential."

"And what will our attitude be towards beauty under the inherent-value paradigm of self-esteem?" I ask.

"Maybe we'll all take the middle ground and just settle on being French fries," Matthew offers. "Our new motto will be 'Potatoes Forever.'" As if cued, everyone's eyes roll in unison.

"Since an external standard of beauty would no longer have relevance," Sarah explains quietly, "then the concept of beauty would have meaning only in relation to the peace and fulfillment of those who were experiencing joy through the realization and expression of inner potential. We would still be concerned with modesty and hygiene, but we would no longer compete with each other to see who could be the most fashionable or stylish. The mirror would lose its power, and we would make peace with our image." Unable to add to her comment, I allow a moment of silence to adorn the image that is inspired by her words.

An Example

Just before Thanksgiving my son Joseph, a second grader, handed me a stack of colorings that he had made at school: two pilgrims, an Indian, and a turkey. With bright eyes he asked where we could hang them so that everyone could see them during the holidays. By way of response, I had three choices. I could impatiently explain that the house already had enough clutter so just please put them away. Or I could take the opposite extreme and praise them as masterpieces that deserved to be framed and put on display in a prominent museum of art. The first would break his heart by discounting the worth of his offering. The second would deceive him through vain flattery, artificially inflate his ego, and create a sense of false pride.

I chose the third option. "Joseph," I said, "it looks like you put a lot of effort into these pictures. I'm sure that we can find a nice place to hang them up where everyone can see them and be reminded of the first Thanksgiving. Thank you for sharing them." Joseph beamed with joy as he was allowed to share his art work and feel that his contribution was valued by his family. More than praise or recognition, what we all need is the opportunity to develop our potential so that we can share it with each other.

SPIRITUAL SOLUTIONS

King Mosiah taught his people "that they should let no pride nor haughtiness disturb their peace" (Mosiah 27:4). He tried to prevent the inevitable social downfall that occurs when people become enmeshed in the vanity of trying to "add value" to their personal worth so that they can rise above each other. Instead he encouraged "that every man should esteem his neighbor as himself" (27:4). Such esteem occurs when we each recognize our unique worth and the worth of others and work together in supportive ways to realize the many potentials with which God has blessed us.

SUMMARY

The inherent-value approach to self-esteem represents an alternative paradigm for understanding and enhancing *true* self-esteem. The definition of self-esteem under this paradigm is "the sense of joy experienced when inherent potential is discovered and realized." The worth of the self arises from the existence of human potential, which is unique, infinitely valuable, and not comparable.

The worth of the self is considered to be inherent and fixed. Nothing we can do will alter the value of the potential that our lives represent. If the potential is realized, the result will be lasting joy. If the potential is left unrealized, the result will be emptiness and nagging dissatisfaction with life. The discovery and realization of potential requires a social system that supports self-discovery and that appreciates human diversity. It requires the diligent pursuit of self-understanding and inner development, rather than the pursuit of vain accomplishments and social applause.

Under this paradigm there are no external standards of beauty, only the inner peace and fulfillment that shines from the eyes of those who are experiencing joy through the realization and expression of inner potential. Enhancing self-esteem as understood in the inherent-value model would do much to reduce many of the social problems we experience today. As we seek to realize true self-esteem in our own lives, we will also be able to support others as they look for the correct path.

CHAPTER NINE

SELF-ESTEEM IS LIKE WHITE COTTON SOCKS

If another person only had in his storehouse of deserved
self-esteem what you had put there, what would he have to
draw upon to sustain him?
—Neal A. Maxwell

THE PARABLE OF THE TALENTS

In a spiritual sense, true self-esteem is exemplified by the parable of the talents from the New Testament. In the parable, three different servants get "talents" from their master. They each receive a different number, perhaps symbolizing that our talents are unique and not comparable to those given to others. Even though the servants start off on unequal footing, each one is expected to multiply the talents that he was given.

When the master returns, he does not judge the servants in relation to each other; instead he judges them individually on the basis of how well they cared for the talents they were given. To those who magnified their talents he says, "Well done thou good and faithful servant: thou hast been faithful over a few things, I will make thee a ruler over many things: enter thou into the *joy* of thy lord" (Matthew 25:14–30; emphasis added).

On the other hand, the servant who did not magnify his talent is called a "wicked and slothful servant" by his lord. The servant is upbraided for not diligently putting his talent to good use and other servants are instructed to "cast the unprofitable servant into outer darkness: [where] there shall be weeping and gnashing of teeth."

The talents portrayed in this parable represent our inner potential, or spiritual gifts. The implication of the parable is that each person has a different set of spiritual gifts that only he or she can develop and express. And like the servants in the parable, we will each be held accountable before our Heavenly Father as to how *we* develop *our* potential. Without reference to the accomplishments or disappointments of others, we will each answer for ourselves, just like the servants in the parable.

If we discover and realize our potential the result will be joy. Not just momentary feelings of happiness or pleasure, but the greatest experience of lasting joy that is possible—even the *joy of the Lord*. On the other hand, if we ignore and waste our potential, the result will be "weeping and gnashing of teeth." If we fail to open and enjoy our spiritual gifts as part of the opportunity afforded by this lifetime, the resulting sense of loss may be one of the greatest disappointments that we will ever face.

THE PARABLE OF THE WHITE COTTON SOCKS

I am reminded of an experience from my youth that partially captures what it would be like to face the Lord with the unhappy task of explaining to him that we buried the talents he gave us and left them hidden and unused. I call it The Parable of the White Cotton Socks.

When I was in eighth grade I tried out for football and actually made the team (as did everyone else who tried out). We lived in southeast Missouri, and the team was coached by a turnip-faced tyrant named Coach K. On the first day of practice, before we had even dressed out, he gathered all the players together and preached a fiery sermon.

"Now boys," he began with a harsh southern accent, "there is only one main rule in this here football club. And that rule is this: You wear your white cotton socks every time you dress out. I repeat: You always wear your white cotton socks." He held up a pair of white cotton socks by way of illustration and then yelled at us like we were new military recruits. "You were *issued* white cotton socks, and you will wear white cotton socks if you are going to play for this ball club." His voice was very loud and he seemed quite worked up. His eyes were bulging.

"Now don't any of you boys come out on this ball field unless you are fully dressed out, complete with white cotton socks. Do I make myself clear?" He was now bellowing at us like a drill sergeant. "You are expected to wear your white cotton socks!"

We all looked at each other, shrugged our shoulders, and dressed out. *What's the big deal about white cotton socks?* I remember thinking to myself. All went well until a few weeks later when I realized, just before practice, that my white cotton socks were not with the rest of my workout clothes. *Oh, no,* I thought. *My mom must have lost them in the wash. Now what am I going to do?*

"Hey, Piekielniak," I hollered to a friend across the locker room, "can I borrow your white cotton socks? I can't find mine."

"Are you kidding?" he replied, "I need my white cotton socks. There's no way I'd go out there without them. Coach K would kill me. Ask someone else."

Other requests for help met with similar results. No one would loan me a pair of white cotton socks. As I saw it, I had three choices: skip practice altogether, wear no socks at all, or wear my navy blue school socks. *What the heck,* I decided. *How big of a deal can it be to not wear white cotton socks for a single day?*

I hadn't been on the practice field more than two seconds before I saw Coach K's eyes dart to my ankles. He immediately stomped toward me, fists clenched, gaining steam like a locomotive. I froze in my tracks, waiting for the force of the oncoming train to sweep me into the next county. "Hawks!" he yelled as he put his angry red face very close to mine, "What have you got on your feet, boy? Huh?"

Shock and terror impaired my power of speech to such an extent that he was compelled to scream out the question again. "I *said*, what have you got on your feet, boy?"

"Socks," I finally whispered.

"I can't hear you," he yelled.

"Socks," I said louder.

"And what color are your 'socks,' Hawks?"

"Blue."

His eyes narrowed and the veins bulged in his neck as his voice became a low hiss. "Were you not issued a pair of clean, white cotton socks at the beginning of this football season, boy?"

"Yes, sir."

"Good. Now would you mind telling me just where your white cotton socks might happen to be, since they are clearly not on your feet where they belong?"

"I think my mom lost them in the laundry," I explained weakly.

"Boys," he yelled angrily at my teammates, "boys, huddle up here around Hawks. Let's go! Move! Move! Move!"

As my teammates quickly assembled in a large group around me, he continued, "There's only one rule in this ball club—you wear your white cotton socks at all times. You *never* show up out here without your white cotton socks on your feet. Did I not make that rule perfectly clear on the first day of practice?"

"You made it perfectly clear, sir," Piekielniak shouted like a dutiful private. I gave him a glare that was intended to cut him in half. He smiled back.

"Well, Hawks here doesn't think he has to live by the same rules as everybody else in this ball club," Coach K continued fiercely. "He thinks that it's just fine to wear pretty blue socks anytime he feels like it. The best excuse he can come up with is that his momma lost his white cotton socks in the laundry." The other players snickered in derision at this comment. "That is pitiful," Coach K continued. "Don't any of you ever come on this ball field and tell me that your momma lost your white cotton socks in the laundry. I will eat you alive."

"No, sir. Never, sir," the other boys answered.

Turning back to me with the full force of his wrath he said, "You are pitiful, boy. You are absolutely pitiful. Now you turn your little behind around and get off this football field. You get out of here now. Go on—get." At this point he started to chase me while hollering at the top of his voice, "I said you get out of here now, boy. Move! Move! Move!"

When I finally reached the safety of home, I tried to explain to my mother about the extreme browbeating that I had taken because I had shown up without my socks. She just smiled and said, "Don't be silly, honey. No one would get that mad just because you didn't have on white cotton socks." I can still see her shaking her head with a you're-just-being-silly smile on her face.

THE MEANING OF THE PARABLE

The meaning of the parable was made clear to me in a dream many years later. I dreamed that I had died and was standing at the gates of heaven. While there, I was met by the angel that decides who can pass through to the other side. The turnip-faced angel looked like Coach K, and he had only one question.

"Where is your potential, Hawks?" he shouted in my face like a platoon leader. "Were you not *issued* some potential? What did you do with the spiritual gifts that you were given? Did you fail to open and share them as you were instructed?"

"I'm not sure," I whispered. I was confused by the fierceness of the questioning, but then I saw Piekielniak standing behind the angel snickering. Suddenly I was terrified as I realized that I couldn't offer any evidence of having any potential or developing any spiritual gifts. They were lost. I knew I was in for it as the purple-blotched face of Angel K contorted into a menacing grimace.

"What's the matter, Hawks? Did your momma lose your potential in the laundry? Is that what happened, boy? Huh?" He was getting more and more angry as he asked each question without receiving an acceptable reply. Finally he just shook his head in disgust and said, "You are pitiful, boy. Now you go on and get out of here and don't you come back until you have some potential. Go on—get." And then he chased me away from heaven, shouting, "Move! Move! Move!" I woke up drenched in sweat, but happy to still be alive and at least for the moment out of the reach of Angel K.

In the parable of the socks, every person was issued a pair of white cotton socks. In life, we have all been issued unique spiritual potential. Just as everyone was expected to wear his socks in the parable, everyone is expected to be "clothed" in his or her potential. That is, they are expected to develop the spiritual gifts and attributes that identify them as children of God. They are expected to accept that their potential is real and recognize that it provides the foundation for who they are and what they can become.

Just as it didn't seem to be that big of a deal to not wear my white cotton socks, it may not seem that critical to discover and realize spiritual potential, especially when there are so many distractions all around us. But I am convinced that there will come a time when we will wish with all the energy of our souls that our potential had been taken seriously and managed wisely. When the moment arrives in which we must answer for the development of our spiritual gifts, we will not be able to borrow potential from a friend. When the Master shows up and asks to see the increase in our talents, others will not be able to loan us theirs. If our potential has not been developed, there will be no way of hiding that fact from him. Just like it was impossible to hide my blue socks.

In the end, our ability to demonstrate that we realized the potential that was given to us will determine our chances for joy in this life and in the life to come. As with the slothful servant, it will be most unpleasant for us if we can offer no evidence of having developed our potential. A browbeating from Coach K will seem mild by comparison.

CAN WE CHANGE OUR WORTH?

The two contrasting versions of self-esteem outlined in chapters seven and eight are underscored by a debate about the changeability of the worth of the self. The debated question asks, "Is there anything that *we* can do to change the value of who or what we are?" As you will remember, the value-added approach to self-esteem argues that we can become more worthwhile through our visible accomplishments and achievements. Conversely, the inherent-value paradigm holds that the value of the self is fixed and unchangeable. Our worth cannot be altered through recognition, success, or personal achievement.

It is important to resolve this debate. One possible answer can be found in the scriptures.

What is our worth?

It is interesting to find seemingly contradictory passages of scripture that attempt to characterize our worth. On the positive side, we read in Psalms that man is "crowned with glory and honor" (Psalm 8:5). In the book of Alma, the prophet Alma declares that "souls are precious" (Alma 31:35). And in the Doctrine and Covenants we read that "the worth of souls is great in the sight of God" (D&C 18:10).

On what could be called the negative side, however, the book of Moses records that we are really nothing more than "dust" (Moses 4:25). The prophet Mormon takes the analogy a step further and says that we are "less than the dust of the earth" (Helaman 12:7). King Benjamin seems to agree by asking us to remember our "own nothingness" (Mosiah 4:11). In obedience to this request the prophet Ammon humbly admits, "Yea, I know that I am nothing" (Alma 26:12).

And so how can souls be "precious," on one hand, and yet even a prophet of God be considered as "nothing," on the other hand? The answer seems to depend on our understanding of what determines our worth and whether we think we can change that worth through our personal efforts.

Our Worth Is a Gift

King Benjamin makes the point that our worth is a gift from God. "In the first place, he hath created you, and granted unto you your lives," he explains. All that we are, and even the breath that we draw, is a gift from God, "for which [we] are indebted unto him" (Mosiah 2:23). Our worth arises from the fact that we are the handiwork of God and that he has endowed us with tremendous spiritual potential, even the potential to become like him. Because of our divine parentage and the spiritual traits that our maker has given us, we are "precious" and "crowned with glory and honor." Because of this doctrine, we know why "the worth of souls is great in the sight of God."

How then do we conclude that we are less than the dust of the earth? First, we must remember that our preciousness does not arise from anything that we have done. It is inherent within us due to our eternal lineage and the spiritual potential which God has seen fit to bestow upon us. We have done nothing. And so when the terms *nothing* and *less than the dust of the earth* are applied to us, it is a reminder that we have done nothing to determine our worth. And further, that we are powerless to alter it.

We Have Nothing to Boast About.

King Benjamin explains that even if we reverence our Father in Heaven and "serve him with all [our] souls yet [we] would be unprofitable servants" (Mosiah 2:21). There is nothing we can do—no achievement so great or act of sacrifice so sublime—that can change the fact that our worth is entirely a gift from God. Even a prophet, someone devoted to the service of his creator, declares himself to be "nothing" in respect to this principle.

King Benjamin explains by saying, "in the first place, he hath created you, and granted unto you your lives, for which ye are indebted unto him. And secondly, he doth require that ye should do as he hath commanded you; for which if ye do, he doth immediately bless you; and therefore hath paid you. And ye are still indebted to him, . . . therefore, of what have ye to boast? Ye cannot even say that ye are even as much as the dust of the earth" (Mosiah 2:23–25).

No matter what fame, glory, wealth, power, status, beauty, or other achievement we attain to in this live, we are indebted for all of it to God and therefore we have nothing to boast about. We must not conclude that it is the strength of our own arm that defines our worth. For no matter how strong our arm, even if we use it in the cause of righteousness, we cannot say that we are even as much as "the dust of the earth."

SPIRITUAL SOLUTIONS

We are precious and of great worth because we are the offspring of deity and have the potential to become like our heavenly parents. And yet we are nothing, even less than the dust of the earth, because we can do nothing of ourselves to add to the worth that God has granted us. Paradoxically, these two principles provide not only the foundation for humility but the foundation for true self-esteem.

The value-added paradigm of self-esteem, promoted by the world around us, would have us believe that external achievements (beauty, wealth, fame, popularity, and so on) define our worth. In the end, this leads to vanity and disappointment as we try to rise above others by measuring up to the external yardsticks that society holds up for us. "Therefore they began to set their hearts upon their riches; yea, they began to seek to get gain *that they might be lifted up one above another*" (Helaman 6:17; emphasis added). This attitude is the source of false pride (as opposed to humility) and it is in relation to this attitude that King Benjamin asks, "of what have ye to boast? Ye cannot say that ye are even as much as the dust of the earth" (Mosiah 2:25).

In contrast, the inherent value paradigm of self-esteem correctly assumes that our value is inherent and unchangeable. Our value is based on our divine pedigree and our God-given potential. The realization of that potential does nothing to change our worth—we will always be indebted to God for that—but it allows us to experience *the joy of the lord,* which is the joy of spiritual growth and development that accompanies the realization of inner potential. The value of the self is not changed, only the chance to experience joy is increased as we realize our potential.

"Men are that they might have joy," (2 Nephi 2:25); the magnification of spiritual gifts bestowed by heaven is the path to this end. When we develop our spiritual potential, our joy as well as our Heavenly Father's is enhanced. In the same way that we experience joy as we see our children make spiritual progress, our Heavenly Father delights in our righteous development.

On the other hand, failure to recognize and develop our spiritual potential will ultimately lead to severe regret and disappointment. Such disappointment can only be characterized by "weeping and gnashing of teeth." And not only do we forfeit our opportunity for joy, but we also deprive our Heavenly Father of the joy that he might have taken in our spiritual growth. This is the likely outcome for those who follow the value-added approach to self-esteem by seeking success, achievement, and recognition, while neglecting the development of their inherent spiritual potential. It will not go well for us if Angel K finds us trying to get into heaven without any evidence that we have developed the spiritual gifts that we were "issued."

If all of God's children would devote their lives to the realization of their unique spiritual potential, then all the gifts of heaven would be expressed upon the earth for our mutual benefit. Such would be a true utopia. This was the case in the years immediately following the visitation of Christ to the Americas. The prophet Mormon explains, "And they had all things in common among them; therefore there were not rich and poor, bond and free, but they were all made free, and partakers of the heavenly gift. And there were no envyings or strife . . . and surely there could not be a happier people . . . they were in one, the children of Christ, and heirs to the kingdom of God. And how blessed were they!" (4 Nephi: 3, 16–18).

But if instead we focus on competing with one another for popularity by striving to realize vain achievements, then our true gifts are lost and all mankind is impoverished. Such would be true desolation. Concerning the decline of the Nephites, the prophet Mormon explains, "The great slaughter which was among them, would not have happened had it not been for . . . the pride of their hearts. And because of . . . their boastings in their own strength, they were left in their own strength; therefore they did not prosper, but were afflicted and smitten, and driven. . . ." (Helaman 4: 11–13).

EXPANDING THE SPHERE OF SPIRITUAL INFLUENCE

In the Parable of the Talents, the servants that multiply their talents not only receive joy but they are given further talents and responsibilities. In other words, the sphere within which their spiritual gifts can exert positive influence continues to expand as they multiply their talents. The Savior taught that, "whosoever will be chief among you, let him be your servant" (Matthew 20:27). It is by recognizing and developing our spiritual gifts that we increase our capacity to serve and minister to one another, and thereby increase our sphere of positive influence.

And it is by recognizing the value of the spiritual gifts that are inherent in each of God's children that we increase our capacity to love one another. This is the key to increasing our ability to express unconditional love as described in chapter six. The ongoing process of recognizing and developing our talents, while valuing and encouraging the talents of others, is part of the process for realizing self-actualization that was envisioned by Maslow.

SUMMARY

The true definition of self-esteem is the realization of joy that occurs as inner potential is recognized and expressed. This is illustrated in the parable of the talents as those servants who magnify their talents, or in other words realize their spiritual potential, are invited to "enter into the joy of the lord." False self-esteem is characterized by the fleeting gratification of vanity that arises from social praise in response to narrowly defined accomplishments. Such gratification often comes at the expense of recognizing and developing spiritual potential. As illustrated in the parable of the talents, the end of this path is "weeping and gnashing of teeth."

The realization of spiritual potential, the foundation of self-esteem, is like white cotton socks. We have been "issued" potential, and only *we* can realize the potential that was given to us. It cannot be borrowed from others. We will be held accountable for it, and if we come up short it will not go well for us. Souls are precious and of great worth to our Heavenly Father. This is because we are his children and are endowed with the potential to become like him.

Humility arises from the understanding that we are of great worth due to our spiritual parentage, but that of ourselves we are nothing. We can do nothing to add to the worth that God has already granted us. This concept is central to true self-esteem. False pride arises from the belief that we can add to our worth through our own achievements. This concept is central to false self-esteem, or vanity.

Utopia would occur if all of our Heavenly Father's children recognized their innate worth and strove to develop their spiritual potential. Desolation occurs when we strive to rise above each other by competing for worldly praise and success.

It is by recognizing and developing our spiritual gifts that we increase our capacity to serve and minister to one another. And it is by recognizing the value of the spiritual gifts that are inherent in each of God's children that we increase our capacity to love one another. The sphere within which our spiritual gifts can exert positive influence continues to expand as we multiply our talents. This is the process of self-actualization as envisioned by Maslow.

THE PURSUIT OF HAPPINESS

To Aristotle, "happiness" was seen as the ultimate goal of human existence. The Greek term for this high objective, for which "happiness" is an imperfect translation, was *eudaimonia*. Aristotle's understanding of the concept of *eudaimonia*, or happiness, was that it was accomplished through *the actualization of a soul with respect to its proper function*. This definition is reminiscent of Maslow's concept of self-actualization.

But before we can adequately discuss the path to self-actualization, or *eudaimonia*, we must first understand all of the forces that either direct us toward the proper function of our soul, or persuade us away from it. In this section we discuss the body and mind as two different forces that may actually push us away from happiness as understood by Aristotle.

CHAPTER TEN

THE NATURAL MAN

Appetite grows the keener by indulgence.
—Benjamin Franklin

Imagine the great philosopher Aristotle, sometime around 340 BC, as he gravely ascends to the top of some sort of raised object—perhaps a stump or a block of granite. After silencing his assembled students by tilting his head slightly to one side and raising a thoughtful eyebrow, he clears his throat and utters a truth:

"More than any thing else," he whispers gravely, "men and women seek happiness."[1]

After nodding their heads and exchanging glances of approval with one another, the students break into applause, shake Aristotle's hand warmly, and then head to the nearest tavern to fully imbibe both the implications of this saying and a stout beverage that might hasten its realization. Forever after, the phrase is repeated often— *"more than anything else, men and women seek happiness."* The expression is no less true for us than it was for Aristotle's students. But how can we achieve the elusive state of happiness for which we seek?

Since Aristotle's day, much has been written on the nature of happiness, and many strategies have been devised over the intervening years that can supposedly lead to its attainment. Yet there are few today that put forth a great deal of effort to seek out and study the ancient philosophies or to challenge the validity of the tactics they reveal. But one's ability to chart an accurate course to happiness, and to successfully navigate safe passage, requires at least a cursory familiarity with the variety of paths from which we must choose.

One of the more interesting philosophers of happiness was Søren Kierkegaard (1813–55), a native of Denmark who eventually became the father of existential philosophy. Kierkegaard was a complex man who more than anything else wanted to lead an authentic, fully involved, actualized life. In his early and most famous writings, Kierkegaard critiques three different approaches or paths to realizing the happiness of which Aristotle spoke. We can label these three paths respectively the aesthetic life, the ethical life, and the spiritual life.[2]

The aesthetic life is consumed by an impulsive quest for sensual gratification, and so it represents the pursuit of happiness at the level of the physical body. The ethical life concerns itself with social correctness and conformity, and thus the pursuit of happiness at the level of the mind. On the other hand, the spiritual life seeks to realize the imperatives of inner faith and spirituality, which represent the pursuit of happiness at the level of the spirit.

Kierkegaard's three different approaches to happiness mirror the elements of the mind, the body, and the spirit that this section of the book attempts to illustrate. All of these forces have profound implications for the pursuit of happiness, and they are therefore worthy of further examination. This chapter deals with the aesthetic life (pursuing happiness at the body level) which is aptly captured by the words "the natural man." Chapters eleven and twelve explore the ethical life (happiness as sought at the mind level).

AESTHETICS AND THE NATURE OF PHYSICAL PLEASURE

After futile attempts to gain the attention of my students by imitating the tilted head and subtle eyebrow manipulations that were no doubt utilized by Aristotle, I give up and resort to storytelling. The description of an exotic scenario at last gains their interest.

"Let's pretend that we are traversing the interior of a remote continent," I suggest, "and that we happen across an untainted tribe of aborigines. Let's assume that since they might be dangerous, we decide to avert potential hostilities by offering them food. We happen to have extra provisions of two items—chocolate bars and celery sticks."

With the satisfied look of one who is in sole possession of esoteric knowledge, I ask, "Should we offer them chocolate, or celery?"

Suspecting a trick question, no one offers a comment until Sarah tentatively says, "Maybe you should give them celery because they are used to natural plant foods, and they have probably never even tasted chocolate. They would be happier with something familiar to them."

"Perhaps," I say. "But if you allowed them to taste both, which would they want more of?" At this point several different views are offered in support of each alternative. After debating the issue and considering several examples, it is generally conceded that chocolate would be preferred. Given time and opportunity, traditional diets generally give way to modern processed food (high fat and high sugar), often with negative consequences. The increasing rate of diet-related diabetes among the Pima Indians of the U.S. offers one example.[3]

If the argument in favor of the chocolate bar requires further support, I refer to the example of my watchdog Seiko. As per his vet's instructions I give Seiko only the highest quality dog food; he never gets table scraps. And so, given his circumstance and upbringing, what will Seiko choose if given the opportunity—a hot dog or the usual brand of dog food to which he is accustomed? Undoubtedly, the class agrees, he will prefer the hot dog.

"But why?" I ask the students.

Even though the words differ slightly, the meaning behind all of the answers is the same—"because the hot dog tastes better."

"Similarly, if provided with a tasters' table of chocolate and

celery," I explain, "the aborigines would soon exhibit a strong preference for chocolate."

Such is the nature of Kierkegaard's *Aesthetic Life*. As a goal in the
pursuit of happiness, one blindly seeks to obtain those things that
most fully gratify the physical senses. In this case, the animal sense of
appetite is more appeased by hot dogs and chocolate than by dog food
and celery, and hence they are selected. It is a simple concept. But
what Kierkegaard was unable to do, given the infancy of biological
and genetic sciences in his day, was to explain why some things were
more appealing to the senses than others.

Likewise, my next question takes much longer for the students to
resolve: "Why do the hot dog or the chocolate taste better than their
less desirable alternatives?"

As I pace before the students, proud of my Socratic line of questioning and wishing that I had a block of granite to wisely stand upon,
they offer a variety of responses. "Because it feels good. It is more
pleasurable. It makes you feel better."

All of these answers, I observe to the class, merely restate the definition of "taste better" (that is, make you feel better, provide pleasure) without adding any insight as to why. "Why does the chocolate
make you feel better, or provide more pleasure, then celery?" I persist.

Kristen, the nurse, eventually proposes that "some foods may taste
better because they offer a survival advantage." As this insight fills
the minds of other students, spontaneous "aaahhs" resonate through
the classroom. Such audible evidences of learning would have made
even Aristotle proud. As we explore the statement further, we come
to the conclusion that biological organisms (humans included) have
genetic programming that rewards the selection of energy dense foods
with sensations of pleasure.[4]

And thus we find the key for understanding the motivating force
behind all aspects of the *Aesthetic Life*. The pursuit of happiness via

the indulgence of sensual pleasure merely represents the intentional gratification of genetically programmed biological urges that serve the singular purpose of enhancing survival.

At a more basic level, we could go back to the primordial soup of prelife earth and consider the strands of DNA that begin to form there. Over time, the strands seem to take on a single purpose— replication. If taken to an extreme level, we could conclude that all living organisms on this planet are simply the result of DNA and genetic material trying to devise better structures and strategies for survival and replication. Physical pleasure, as felt by humans, is merely a genetically programmed reward for behaving in a way that enhances the likelihood that genes will get passed on to the next generation. It has no deeper meaning, at least at the body level.

PLEASURE AND FOOD SELECTION

As noted previously, it seems probable that the amount of pleasure we derive from different foods (how good they taste) correlates directly with the survival advantage they offer. As we consider the history of the human species, it becomes clear that it is characterized by regular, life-threatening episodes of famine. (The average life expectancy ranged between 35 to 45 years for most of human history, rising above 50 only during the 20th century). Perhaps even more than war or disease, it was the unreliable supply of food that posed the greatest threat to survival and genetic replication during much of human history.[5]

Those individuals who exhibited a genetically programmed preference for energy dense foods (chocolate tasting better to them than, say, celery) tended to have a better chance for surviving the famine because they stored the extra energy in the form of fat. The genes that provide pleasurable rewards for energy dense food selection were passed on, and we inherited them. As such, we have a genetically programmed, biological preference for high fat, high sugar (energy dense) foods. Such a preference has never posed a problem, until recently, as energy dense foods were not consistently and readily available to the average person. Since they were a rarity, they would be feasted upon whenever conditions allowed and thereby help the individual store much-needed fat reserves.

For good or evil, I have noticed that the "feasting" gene is alive and well within me—nor do I seem to be alone. Research has shown that the amount of sugar and fat in the American diet increased steadily from the turn of the century until the 1950s (in direct correlation with availability), where it has remained relatively stable for the past half-century. We seem to have reached a saturation point where we get almost 40 percent of calories from fat (double the recommended amount) and 20 percent of calories from sugar (again, double the recommended amount).[6]

PLEASURE AND ACTIVITY LEVEL

Again, the history of the human species makes it clear that significant energy expenditure (hard work) was generally necessary for survival. Whether the hard work took the form of hunting, child rearing, farming, or gathering, humans could not survive—genes could not be passed on, the survivability of the next generation could not be ensured—unless large amounts of energy were expended in active labor. Yet, too much energy expenditure, in relation to the amount of energy consumed and stored, placed individuals at risk for death during famines. It is therefore conceivable, even probable, that there is genetic programming that rewards energy-saving inactivity with a sense of pleasure.

We would not have to poll too many teenagers at my house, for example, before it became clear that for many individuals there is a certain amount of pleasure associated with lounging around (often in front of a TV), as opposed to willfully engaging in strenuous physical activity (like mowing the lawn). If given a choice, most people will live sedentary lives as opposed to making a conscious decision to be more active. On average, the level of inactivity has risen during this century (in direct proportion to the decreased need for physical labor to sustain life) to the point that 60 percent of the population does not get enough activity to obtain a health benefit.[7] In fact, the percentage of the population that remains active does so primarily because of the nature of their occupation (being a roofer as opposed to an accountant), not because of conscious efforts to increase activity.

Given the increased availability and consumption of energy dense foods, and the declining levels of physical activity, it is not surprising that the prevalence of obesity has continued to rise steadily during this century, to the point that one out of four Americans is now considered obese. One does not need to look further than genetically predisposed changes in diet composition and activity level to explain the "epidemic" of obesity in the U.S.[8]

PLEASURE, GENES AND REPRODUCTIVE STRATEGIES

The Female Strategy

"If the genetically programmed purpose of biological organisms is to behave in a way that enhances DNA replication," I ponder, "then what is the reproductive strategy of female humans?"[9]

The obvious answers are soon expressed—"To have sex. To make babies." My eyebrows, carefully raised to indicate skepticism, reveal a lack of satisfaction with the responses. "Well, what then?" they ask. Although I may be taking my Aristotle imitations too far, I offer a new line of Socratic questioning.

"While it is true that they must have sex and make babies, that is not enough. They must see that their babies grow to reproductive maturity." I ask them to imagine a woman, a member of a tribe far back in the primeval days of human history. "It may be relatively easy for her to have babies," I note, "but what does she have to do to see that her babies arrive at adulthood so that her DNA can continue to replicate for many generations to come? Does she need help?"

Even though it is difficult for my modern students to appreciate or accept, I finally coax out of them the response, "she has to have a mate to protect and provide for her."

By small increments and tortured degrees, we arrive at the conclusion that the reproductive strategy of females, genetically, is to attract a mate who is a good provider and protector and who offers long-term emotional commitment to her and her offspring. As my audience is mostly female, and knowing that my next line of reasoning will lead us into dangerous waters, I proceed cautiously.

"So, what might our female of bygone days offer in exchange for protection and long-term commitment?" A few faces turn red. I become conscious of some angry glares. No one says anything. I clear my throat nervously, and try to smile. "Any ideas, anybody?"

Finally Brittany breaks the silence with a quiet voice full of thinly veiled sarcasm. "Sex? Is that what you're trying to get us to say?" My enthusiastic smile, raised eyebrows, and wrinkled forehead clearly indicate a correct response, but no one seems particularly pleased or supportive. In fact I am aware of a certain tension in the air.

To avert a quarrel, I launch into a lengthy explanation that up to this point we have been talking only about the *Aesthetic Life*. The genetically programmed, biological life. The natural man. The life motivated by sensual pleasure. I assure them that there are other dimensions of humanity that will also be discussed (that is, the ethical life and the spiritual life). With the air somewhat cleared, we continue.

"Yes," I proceed, "sex. At the *body* level, females offer sex to males in exchange for commitment and protection. There we have said it, and from a biological perspective it is true." While many roll their eyes and murmur in disapproval, mutiny seems to have been forestalled. "Accordingly," I continue bravely, "women compete with one another on the basis of sexual attractiveness. Put a group of women in a room with each other and their first response will be to evaluate the sexual attractiveness of the other women in relation to each other and to themselves. A woman can tell you immediately how any other woman she knows rates on a scale of 1 to 10 in terms of sexual attractiveness." No one is happy about my pronouncements, but several sheepish grins indicate that at least for some an inner truth has been exposed.

The Male Strategy

"A young woman once asked me," I reminisce to the class, "if I thought another man was physically attractive. After pondering the question, and the man, I remarked sincerely that I did not know. She indicated that she had asked other men the same question and received similar responses. After conceding that women can readily offer an opinion on the attractiveness of other woman, she concluded that men, like women, actually did have opinions about the attractiveness of other men, but they were afraid to say so because they were homophobic."

The class enthusiastically agrees with the young woman's assessment, and the spotlight quickly turns from the carnal female to focus its glare upon imperfect man. "What about men," someone asks; "what is their reproductive strategy?"[10]

Once I turn the question back to the class for an answer, it is not long in forthcoming. "Sex. They want to have sex with as many women as possible in order spread their DNA around." Matthew is the only member of the class that seems able to accept this proposition without resentment. For others in the class, the observation is followed with disgusted moans and the exclamation "Why do we even mess with them?"

"Exactly the point," I quickly affirm; "why mess with them? It is this attitude on the part of women that makes life difficult for men. As the predator male roams the countryside he finds that women are not amenable to his desire for sex—unless what?"

"Unless he offers long-term commitment and physical support in exchange!" the class says with one voice.

"Yes, and so men compete with each other on the basis of personality characteristics—dependability, commitment, and supportiveness," I explain. "And on the basis of the ability to provide—physical prowess, signs of success in accumulating wealth, and social status. Several studies have shown that women rate a man's attractiveness in terms of personality and status more often than pure physical appearance. For men it is the opposite. Female attractiveness is rated almost completely in terms of physical parameters."

Referring back to the story of the young woman, I dismiss her conclusion that homophobic males secretly judge each other on the basis of physical attractiveness. Instead I offer the insight that men do indeed rate each other, but on a different scale that somehow measures personality status and ability to provide, not sexual attractiveness. There are many thoughtful expressions as the class tries to assimilate this perspective that, for many, is new. But not all are convinced.

Pleasure, the Mirror, and the Pursuit of Happiness

I summarize the discussion on reproductive strategy by noting that the desire to feel attractive is merely a biological urge, not an indicator of "happiness." Brittany, the prom queen, corrects me by saying, "Oh yeah, well I lost weight and it felt great to have guys drive by and whistle at me." The tide of opinion rapidly swells in favor of her position. Some even applaud.

Hoping to regain momentum, I pull out all the stops. "Yes," I concede, "that would feel great. But for those who use cocaine, it also feels great. Pleasure," I caution, placing a finger to my lips for dramatic emphasis and then lowering my voice, "is not the same as happiness. 'Feeling great' is not the same as 'finding joy.'" I take some satisfaction in the distracted murmurs this observation produces. Outright mutiny has again been postponed.

Brain Chemistry

Kierkegaard correctly identified the eventual outcome of pleasure-seeking that characterizes the aesthetic life. "See him in his season of pleasure," Kierkegaard observed; "did he not crave for one pleasure after another?" While Kierkegaard was able to depict the obsessions and addictions of those who pursued the aesthetic life, the inadequacy of scientific progress in his day prevented him from fully explaining the reason that craving and dependency were inevitable. I, on the other hand, have no such handicap. "Brain chemistry," I explain to the class as I knowingly tap my forehead, "is the answer to our dilemma." It turns out that taking cocaine, and being whistled at, may not be that different.

The sensation of physical pleasure is associated with changes in neurotransmitter levels (for example, dopamine and serotonin) in the medial forebrain bundle, part of the limbic system within the brain that controls emotional response and feelings of pleasure. The sensation of pleasure can be obtained by either engaging in behaviors that conform to requisite genetic programming, or by artificially stimulating the medial forebrain bundle (with drugs or electrical stimulation), and thereby producing a similar change in neurotransmitter activity.[11]

During much of human history, electrical stimulation of the brain and the use of psychoactive drugs were not options for obtaining pleasure. The remaining behavioral options, such as food, sex, and leisure could be indulged in only irregularly. For most individuals, they were scarce commodities. The implication is that the neurotransmitters associated with pleasure were not in danger of being depleted, over used, or thrown out of balance. Each time the desired behavior could be engaged in, a predictable sensation would follow, and then the brain would have ample time to return to normal neurotransmitter levels before the next experience of pleasure could occur.

Pleasure-Seeking and Addiction

For the citizens of modern society, however, there are fewer limitations on rapidly repeated episodes of physical pleasure. It can be indulged in at will and may take a variety of forms—food, drugs, sex, gambling, and lounging around among the rest. Being unused to such an abundance of pleasure, our brains try to seek a new balance or homeostasis that includes the presence of the pleasure-seeking behavior. The process can eventually lead to craving, obsession, addiction, and dependence.[12]

"How do you feel when you eat your very favorite food," I ask by way of illustration, "especially if you are very hungry and you haven't had this particular food for a long time?"

"It feels really good," Matthew explains hungrily. "Can we have a snack break?"

"And once you get going, when do you stop eating your favorite food?" I ask without dignifying Matthew's question with a response. "Do you ever overeat?"

Knowing that they do—that we all do—I continue to question. "And how do you feel when you overeat? How do you feel after you've eaten at your favorite buffet—to the point that you need help walking out to the car? How do you feel when the exit has to be enlarged with heavy machinery in order for you to pass through?"

"It feels really bad," Matthew says. "Never mind about the break."

"Why is it," I wonder out loud, "that pleasure, when freely indulged in, is often followed by a mood that is worse than the one we started with?" If we were to graph repeated experiences of even more intense pleasure, say smoking crack cocaine, it might look something like this:

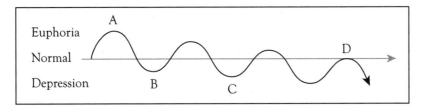

The horizontal line represents our average mood—not particularly happy or sad. Initially, the behavior or drug use results in feelings of euphoria or intense pleasure. Eventually the pleasure peaks (point A), and the following mood is often lethargic or even depressed (point B). Part of the explanation may be that the brain tries to maintain a balance of neurotransmitters (homeostasis), in spite of conditions (pleasurable behavior or drug use) that cause a rush of neurotransmitters in higher than usual levels. Suddenly, the behavior or drug use stops, the brain has overcompensated, and it is now out of balance on the depressed side (point B). Before the brain can normalize, the process is repeated.

The person who relies on pleasure as a substitute for genuine happiness deals with the subsequent depression (or boredom or pain) by again seeking out pleasure—"did he not crave for one pleasure after another." This time, however, he starts out at a slightly depressed state (point B) and reaches a less intense high, which again concludes with even greater depression (point C). As the cycle continues, pleasure-seeking becomes the only escape from despair and misery. It continues to be sought after, even though it no longer provides euphoria, but at best becomes a means for returning to any sense of normalcy (point D).

A FINAL COMMENT ON THE AESTHETIC LIFE

As conceptualized by Kierkegarrd, the *Aesthetic Life* is characterized by the "sensuous immediate." It represents an unexamined life that is lived for the pleasure of the moment without deeper reflection on motivation or consequence. But according to Kierkegaard, this life was ultimately doomed to boredom, despair, and (most importantly) an absence of unique identity. This is because personal identity cannot be formed without breaking free of mindless groping for pleasure and developing a higher aspiration for life that is based on commitment to ideals and adherence to beliefs—both of which are absent at the sensual level of the body.

"The *Aesthetic Life* becomes characterized by dependency, craving, and addiction. The more one comes to rely on physical pleasure to feel good about oneself," I try to explain to Brittany, "the more likely one is to become reliant on pleasure for experiencing even the most basic feelings of normalcy, much less euphoria and the less likely one is to ever achieve real happiness. The pleasure of looking good may be as addictive as the pleasure of cocaine. Once the destructive nature of the *Aesthetic Life* is understood, however, we are free to break away from it and move on to more meaningful aspirations." The day was not yet mine, but I had at least gained her attention—and her supporters were wavering.

SPIRITUAL SOLUTIONS

The *Aesthetic Life*, lived at the body level, is characterized by trying to obtain happiness from physical pleasure. Unfortunately, physical pleasure is nothing more than a biological reward for behavior that enhances genetic survival. The more that pleasure is sought as a way to feel good (euphoria), the more likely it is to end in obsession and dependence as brain chemistry begins to depend on the behavior (or drug) in order to function at normal levels.

Obesity is primarily the result of genetic programming that rewards leisure and the consumption of energy dense foods with pleasure. Given our social environment, a rising prevalence of obesity is to be expected. At the same time, strong genetic programming rewards feelings of sexual attractiveness with pleasure. The desire for approval from the mirror has an aggressive genetic component. When we live life at the body level we are in for torment: the necessity of being increasingly thin in order to derive pleasure from "feeling attractive" is in direct conflict with biological urges that favor increasing weight gain.

Seeking happiness through physical pleasure, or the *Aesthetic Life,* is perhaps the orientation that is condemned in the concept of "the natural man." "For the natural man is an enemy to God . . . and will be, forever and ever, unless he yields to the enticings of the Holy Spirit, and putteth off the natural man" (Mosiah 3:19). The *Aesthetic Life* is a false path for obtaining the happiness of which Aristotle spoke. The pleasure that rewards the achievement of "good looks" is deceptive and potentially destructive, especially if one seeks it as a reliable source for obtaining happiness.

SUMMARY

The *Aesthetic Life* involves a pursuit of "happiness" that is primarily characterized by impulsive attempts to indulge in sensual pleasure. This is the goal of "the natural man," who "is an enemy to God" (Mosiah 3:19). Sensual pleasure is a genetically programmed response to behaviors that enhance the probability that DNA can successfully replicate. At the biological level, pleasure has no other meaning or purpose. Since genes have no awareness of the higher concept of human happiness, they do not program feelings of pleasure in order to promote it.

In relation to body size and appearance, we have genetic programming that pleasurably rewards the selection of energy dense foods and inactivity. Hence, biologically, we have programming that very strongly favors obesity—especially given a social environment where energy dense foods are readily available and sedentary occupations are the norm. At the same time, females have very strong biological programming that encourages competition on the basis of sexual attractiveness (socially defined in terms of thinness). For those who live their life at the body level, the result is constant frustration as these two biological urges are in direct competition with each other.

When we follow our genetic programming and succeed in the competition to be attractive, we are rewarded with physical pleasure (not happiness). It *feels good* to *look good* because we have conformed our behavior to meet the genetic demands for receiving pleasure, not because looking a certain way has anything to do with real happiness.

Physical pleasure and happiness are two different, largely unrelated, concepts. As such, the pursuit of happiness via the realization of sensual pleasure is a false path. Instead, those who pursue happiness by following the *Aesthetic Life,* will often end their journey in the chains of obsession, addiction, dependency, intensified cravings for more sensual pleasure, and hopeless frustration. "See him in his season of pleasure, did he not crave for one pleasure after another?"

The *Aesthetic Life* results in pain but, above all, boredom. In the end, the search for novelty in sensual pleasure leads to the threshold of despair. By analyzing Kierkegaard's concept of the *Ethical Life* in the next two chapters we begin to understand why a society that is biologically prone to obesity would ironically choose thinness as the standard for feminine beauty.

CHAPTER ELEVEN

THE ETHICAL LIFE

A great part of the miseries of mankind are brought upon them by false estimates they have made of the value of things.
—Benjamin Franklin

As the next session of class begins, I place a tattered cap upon my head, button up an old vest, and wrap a prayer shawl around my waist. With a milk pail in one hand, and while imitating the provincial dialect of nineteenth-century Russia, I stroll among the startled students and recite from memory the following lines:

"A fiddler on the roof. Sounds crazy, eh? Here in our little village of Anatevka, you might say that everyone of us is a fiddler on the roof—trying to scratch out a pleasant, simple tune without breaking his neck. You may ask, why do we stay up there if it's so dangerous? Well, we stay because Anatevka is our home. And how do we keep our balance? That I can tell you in one word. Tradition.

"Because of our traditions, we have kept our balance for a very long time. Here in Anatevka we have traditions for everything—how to sleep, how to eat, how to work, how to wear our clothes. For instance, we always keep our heads covered and wear a little prayer shawl. This shows our constant devotion to God. How did this tradition get started? Well, I'll tell you. I don't know. But it's a tradition. And because of our traditions everyone of us knows who he is and what God expects him to do."

As I conclude the opening lines of *Fiddler on the Roof,* the students are unsure as to whether they should clap or simply maintain the embarrassed silence. Silence prevails.

SOCIAL CONFORMITY AND HAPPINESS

"The *Ethical Life*," I finally explain while shedding the guise of Tevya, "was meant by Kierkegaard to represent the life that conforms to social expectation. This stage of life rises above the visceral motivation of the *Aesthetic Life* by concerning itself with adherence to social ideals. But even then, it is a life that is examined only deeply enough to reveal discrepancies between personal behavior and cultural tradition. The model for the *Ethical Life* is the good citizen—the man or woman who not only adapts to social norms, but seeks to epitomize them. It is expected that social conformance, the benchmark of the *Ethical Life*, will reward the conformer with the prize of happiness."

The *Ethical Life* is all about the mind, rather than the body. The mind represents what we think, and what we think largely determines how we behave. We are too often unaware of the profound influence that social tradition exerts on the quality of our thoughts and ultimately on our behavior.

"Tevya, for example," I say, gesturing towards the students with my milk pail, "unquestioningly judges the correctness of all behaviors—sleep, meals, work, dress, marriage—against the standard of cultural tradition, even though he can't explain where his traditions came from. The central tension of the story wavers between conformity to social tradition, on the one hand, and allegiance to the urgings of the heart, on the other. In some cases, tradition is flexible enough to forgive aberration, as in the marriage of the first two daughters on the basis of personal preference, rather than parental arrangement. In other cases it remains rigid, even to the point of disinheriting a child, as in the marriage of the third daughter outside of the faith. Tevya does not question the correctness of tradition; he simply follows it. Is Tevya's conformity to social norms (the *Ethical Life*) ultimately a source of happiness, or a source of pain—or both?" It is an important question.

How shall we judge the appropriateness of conforming to social expectations as a path for obtaining happiness? We have already concluded that our genes do not program sensations of physical pleasure as a means to personal happiness. Likewise, we might ask if it is the explicit goal of societies to create social norms and cultural traditions that when followed maximize the happiness of individuals—or do some societies have other, less pure motives?

THE ANTS AND THE BALLOON

As a class we explore this question in the form of an analogy called *The Ants and the Balloon*. "Imagine that we are all ants out in a meadow enjoying a nice day when one of us, perhaps Holly, spots a bright yellow object high up in the sky. In reality the object is a balloon," I explain to the students, "but since we haven't had any experience with balloons, we don't know that. For several minutes we ponder as to what the bright yellow object might be. We rule out the sun, because we can see it elsewhere in the sky. Eventually, one of us, perhaps Sarah, will say, 'maybe it's honey. It looks like it might be honey.' A murmur runs through our ranks at this idea. We do have experience with honey, and we like it. Suddenly, Brittany breaks from the rest of the ants, sprints over to the string hanging down from the balloon, and starts climbing rapidly. What will the rest of us ants do?"

"I'm not letting Brittany get all of the honey," Carol says. "I'd be right behind her."

"Exactly," I agree. "Afraid of missing out on the golden orb of honey, each ant would leap on to the string and begin the long climb up. We don't know for sure how long it will take to climb the string or what we will find at the top, but since everyone else is doing it, we make the climb with the rest. Unfortunately, the climb is long and hard. It takes us most of our short, ant lives to get to the top. We get hot, tired, dirty, hungry, and more miserable the higher we go, and so we begin to claw our way over the top of each other so that we can get there first. Some get pushed off the string. Some of us unfairly hitch a ride on the back of other ants. But finally, Brittany gets to the golden orb of honey first. She opens her large mandible jaws to scoop in the first delicious bite of honey, but what happens instead?"

"The balloon pops," the real Brittany says sadly.

"Exactly. It pops because it is full of helium, not honey, and we all come tumbling down to the earth confused and disappointed. The entire energy of our lives was spent climbing a string that led to nowhere, and now it's time to die."

SOCIETY AND THE BALLOON

"Let us consider our own antlike society," I suggest. "Based on what we see all around us in the media, advertisements, and other expressions of our cultural tradition, how would our society fill in the blank of the following statement? You will be happy when you _____."

"Get rich," Carol says. "Become attractive," Brittany adds with a toss of her hair. Other students contribute other comments. "Have talent. Gain power. Achieve social status. Obtain the right possessions—house, cars, boats, pool. Earn prestige. Get the right career. Become famous." I draw a circle on the board and invite the students to imagine that the circle is a large, yellow balloon floating high in the sky. We allow the deluge of responses to flow into and inflate the *balloon of happiness*.

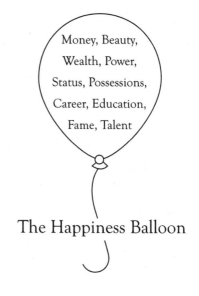

Money, Beauty, Wealth, Power, Status, Possessions, Career, Education, Fame, Talent

The Happiness Balloon

140

"Which of the things in the balloon did Teyva think would bring him happiness ?" I wonder out loud.

"If I were a rich man," someone sings. "Wealth," agrees another student.

"Would it spoil some vast eternal plan," I ask in Tevya's voice, "if I were a wealthy man?" And then with more emotion, and while gazing up at heaven, I say, "If being wealthy is a curse, may the Lord smite me with it!"

"Tevya wanted to be rich," I observe. "Like many of us, he thought it would make him happy. As in our culture, his tradition held that wealth was a virtue. He was living the *Ethical Life*." Taking a hard look at my students, I ask them, "Are any of us living the *Ethical Life?* Which of the things in the balloon do you think will make you most happy?"

"What about education?" I ask as I place the final word in the balloon. "Won't you be happy when you '*get your degree*'?" My tone turns somewhat fierce and accusatory. "Isn't the reason that you are in school so that you can obtain the precious scrap of paper that will increase your ability to obtain a larger piece of the 'happiness' pie? Isn't the reason that you are in this room right now so that you can jump through one more hoop that will bring you that much closer to completing your degree, making you more qualified for the 'right career,' which in turn is sought primarily for the purpose of gaining money, power, prestige, romance, and possessions?"

Before anyone has a chance to call 911, I finally break down and make a confession. "I thought I would be happy if I could just get a doctoral degree," I explain. "I really believed that it would make me more worthwhile. No one in the history of my family had ever gotten a Ph.D. Few had even gone to college. It took me ten years in all. Ten years on the string struggling with the other ants to see who could get to the top first. Everything else in life had to wait until I reached the golden orb of education. We had two children and lived in a miserable one-bedroom apartment with big cockroaches. The children slept on a hide-a-bed in the living room. I was always gone. My family suffered."

The tone of my voice is softened by sad memories. "I tried to convince my wife that it was for her and the kids, but I really knew that I was doing it to gratify my own pride." Trying to smile, I continue, "I dedicated my life to the Ph.D. God and jumped through the education hoops as quickly and gracefully as an armadillo. Even so, I finally graduated as the valedictorian from the College of Physical Education at Brigham Young University and gave a nice speech at the graduation ceremonies. As I stood there, basking in the applause at the end of my address (thinking that at last I was somebody), it felt very good."

"I've heard that cocaine feels good too," remarks Brittany, the attractive young woman who likes to be whistled at.

I smile at her comment, partly because I am glad that she has internalized my earlier point and can now apply it to other situations, and partly to hide the emotions that are rapidly rising to the surface. I am unable to mask their effect on my voice as I express sincere regret. "It was the day after graduation that I realized that the degree had not changed the person that I was. As I walked down the street no one made way for me, no one asked for an autograph, and no one expressed awe at my accomplishments. My sense of inadequacy and all of my fears continued unabated. My relationship with my family was never worse. The education balloon had popped, and I had fallen back to the earth wounded and bewildered."

I have seldom been able to prevent tears from filling my eyes as the image of my young daughter fills my mind and I explain that "there is only one time that you can hold hands with your three-year-old daughter, walk down a country lane, watch the sun set, and pick a flower for Mom—and that's when she's three years old." After a pause, I am able to confess, "I missed that time, and I will always miss it." My voice probably takes on a bitter edge as I pronounce, "There was nothing in the balloon that could make up for what I missed."

A SPECTRAL WARNING ABOUT THE BALLOON

My mind transports me from the classroom to the darkened stage of a local theatre. A scene from the play *A Christmas Carol* is in progress. The ghost of Jacob Marley is warning Ebeneezer Scrooge of his wicked ways when Scrooge tries to pacify him by saying, "But Jacob, you always were a good man of business."

"Business!" Jacob roars, "Business?! Mankind was my business. Mercy, charity, forbearance, the common good were all my business. The comings and goings of my trade were but a drop of water in the comprehensive ocean of my business. Business! In life I failed my business. I drove it to bankruptcy." As he prepares to leave Scrooge, Jacob hauntingly warns him that, "*no space of regret can make amends for one life's opportunity misused.*"

As I turn wild eyed back to my students, I express my remorse with the same rage and terror that tortured Marley's voice, "My speech at graduation," I rasp, "was a humbug. Education?" I yell, "Hah! Mankind was my education. My wife, my friends, my Church, companionship with my children—were all my education. The comings and goings of my lessons were but a drop of water in the comprehensive ocean of my education. Education?! I failed at my education. I drove it to bankruptcy." At last I sigh, the emotion draining out of me, and explain that "the time I spent on the string now represents *one of life's opportunities misused*, one for which *no space of regret can make ammends.*"

It takes a few moments for the class to process the meaning of my personal story, and a few moments for me to smooth down the few hairs that weren't torn out during my rantings. At last, perhaps in an attempt to lighten the mood, Sarah asks the obvious question, "But can't education be a good thing?"

"Yes," I admit with a warm smile, "a very good thing. In fact, any of the things in the balloon *might* be good things."

"Then, I'm confused," she replies quietly.

THE TRUE NATURE OF THE HAPPINESS BALLOON

I ask the students to help me make a list of all the things that our items in the balloon have in common. At first the response is slow, as they wonder what I am looking for, but eventually a variety of insightful answers come forth.

"They are all external, outside of us. They are often temporary. In many respects they appeal to physical pleasure. They mostly represent ease and convenience. They represent a destination—you'll be happy when you get somewhere. They can all be taken away. They are often pursued for self-gratification."

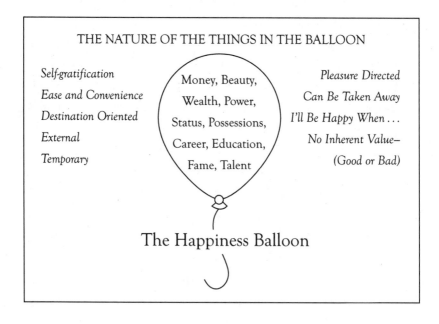

THE NATURE OF THE THINGS IN THE BALLOON

Self-gratification
Ease and Convenience
Destination Oriented
External
Temporary

Money, Beauty, Wealth, Power, Status, Possessions, Career, Education, Fame, Talent

Pleasure Directed
Can Be Taken Away
I'll Be Happy When . . .
No Inherent Value–
(Good or Bad)

The Happiness Balloon

In addition to their comments, I further note that "the things in the happiness balloon have no inherent value. They are neither good, nor bad, of themselves. The value they take on becomes a function of why they are pursued. In our analogy, the yellow balloon had no value good or bad, until it was falsely pursued as a source of life sustaining honey. At that point it became the inspiration for wasted lives. Likewise, if we seek things in the happiness balloon with the expectation that if obtained they will confer happiness, then we are as misguided as the ants. The things in the balloon will become the inspiration for a frustrated life.

"If instead, they are sought as part of a balanced life with a full understanding of how they can be used as tools for a higher purpose, then it is a different matter. In such a case many of the things in the balloon can be put to good use. Even education can be a very good thing—unless it is obsessively pursued as a means for enhancing personal glory. Then the effort is wasted as surely as if it had been spent climbing a string in search of a yellow orb of honey. It all depends on why the things in the balloon are sought and what we hope to gain from them. Too often, our desire is personal gratification, pleasure, vanity, or greed. If so, we are doomed to the same fate as the ants.

"How much 'happiness' do those things really confer on those who seek after them blindly, like ants?" I ask. "Do wealth, fame, career success, talent, beauty, or education, of themselves, convey happiness? Is the possession or absence of these things a reliable predictor of happiness in the lives of people in our country? Do we have to look very far to find individuals who possess most of the things in the balloon, yet who are miserable? Has there ever been a nation in the history of the world that has had more of the things in the balloon than we have right now?" My face reddens as I get warm and self-righteously demand to know whether or not we, as a nation, "have also achieved the highest levels of life satisfaction and happiness in the history of the world? Or do our social norms and cultural traditions betray us," I ask at last, "in our search for personal happiness?"[1]

I try to calm myself as I answer my own questions and observe to the class that even among those who possess most of the things in the balloon there are high levels of depression, drug and alcohol abuse, sexual addiction, and suicide. Even as our country has amassed tremendous wealth and possessions, increases in the rates of violent crime, suicide, psychological disorders, and drug abuse have ironically kept pace.

"Why do the things in the balloon fail to provide long-term life satisfaction and happiness," I probe. "What happens," and this is the critical question I explain, "after we obtain something in the balloon?"

"It feels good," says Brittany. She says this without tossing her hair—a first.

"Yes," I say, dragging the word out like a dirge. "But how do you feel *after* the initial pleasure of say, being attractive, wears off." I know I am on sensitive ground, and I am apprehensive about what her response might be.

"You at first fill empty and bored, and maybe depressed or afraid—but always insecure," she continues slowly. "You're surprised and wonder why the good feeling didn't last as long as you thought it would. You decide that maybe if you can become even more attractive, then everything will be okay and the good feeling will stay." She seems to be coming to new personal insights even as she expresses them.

"Even though you know it won't last, you're afraid of life without a way to feel good. You keep trying to look even better. You depend on your looks to define you. You worry that you might lose your looks." She pauses, and her voice begins to betray her emotions. "Finally, even looking your very best fails to makes you feel good any more, because you're so worried that even your best isn't good enough. Anyway, how you look on the outside doesn't really make you feel good about yourself on the inside. Sometimes you feel like it's all a big game, or a big lie. And then you have to go after something else in the balloon and hope that it will last longer. It never ends, and you are never really happy."

We discuss her response and relate it back to the pleasure-seeking mode of the *Aesthetic Life* and conclude that in many ways, our society has tried to convince us that the path to happiness ends in the arms of pleasure. Living the *Ethical Life*, as defined and promoted by our social culture, has almost merged with living the *Aesthetic Life*. Our most recognizable social norm is the desire for immediate self-gratification through physical pleasure-seeking.

Culture and Beauty

Just as we have found a sense of peace as a class, Brittany creates chaos by adding a postscript. "But no matter what anyone else thinks, I just like to have thin thighs for my own sake—for me," she explains. "I don't really care what society thinks. I just like to have thin thighs."

Before I have a chance to attempt a reply, Holly, the overweight young woman on the front row erupts. She doesn't talk much in class, but when she does there is a reason. "Would you like skinny thighs if you lived in a society that thought people with skinny thighs were ugly, stupid, lazy pigs?" she yells. "Would you still like them *then*, just for your own sake?"

Before it comes to blows, I step between the women and offer a sincere opinion. "If we were all born and raised in a social vacuum we might still be concerned with personal cleanliness and hygiene, but judgments about the value of different sizes of body parts would probably not be of much concern to us. It really is the value that society places on the size of one's thighs that makes it matter to us."

For the same reason that Tevya was obsessed with adhering to his traditions, we feel compelled to conform to social norms. Social norms are often the only guide that people have in judging the appropriateness of behavior and in deciding which path will lead to happiness. It feels safe and secure, on the one hand, and on the other hand you may be ostracized if you fail to conform. It is also a convenient way to relieve ourselves of the responsibility of figuring out how to be happy on our own.

We wonder that Tevya could be so controlled by tradition as to disinherit his own daughter. Yet we are blind to the social strings of our own culture that cause us to jump on cue, just as predictably as puppets, into a fire whose hotness we refuse to question, or that send us on a life-long climb up a string that drains our energy and leads us nowhere.

THE NATURE OF THE STRING

Referring the class back to the analogy of the ants and the balloon I ask, "What does the string represent?"

"It merely represents the means by which the supposed honey can be obtained," Sarah offers.

After more questions and answers about the nature of the string, we conclude that the climb up the string has no other value than the means to get to the honey. Nothing else positive comes of the time spent on the string. We will try to get up it as fast as we can, with as little pain and inconvenience as possible. Our time on the string will be unpleasant, tiring, and boring, so we will minimize it as much as possible, maybe even to the point of hitching a ride on someone else's back, and then climbing ahead of them at the last moment.

"If the balloon represents attractiveness, and we are people instead of ants, then what does the string represent?" I continue.

After a pause, the answers come, "dieting and exercising to lose weight, cosmetics, make-overs, hair treatments, diet pills, plastic

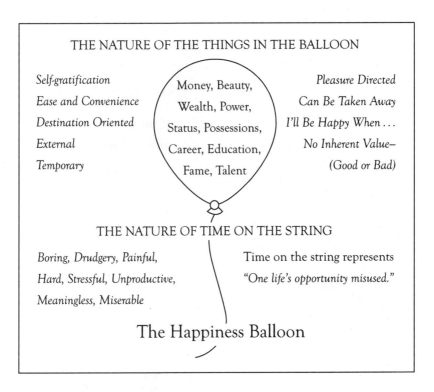

THE NATURE OF THE THINGS IN THE BALLOON

Self-gratification
Ease and Convenience
Destination Oriented
External
Temporary

Money, Beauty,
Wealth, Power,
Status, Possessions,
Career, Education,
Fame, Talent

Pleasure Directed
Can Be Taken Away
I'll Be Happy When . . .
No Inherent Value–
(Good or Bad)

THE NATURE OF TIME ON THE STRING

Boring, Drudgery, Painful,
Hard, Stressful, Unproductive,
Meaningless, Miserable

Time on the string represents
"One life's opportunity misused."

The Happiness Balloon

surgery, tanning salons, liposuction—in short, anything that helps us get to the beauty balloon first, fastest, and easiest so that we can have the exclusive privileges that we think beauty affords."

"What happens when the first ant gets to the balloon and tries to get the honey out?"

"The balloon pops, the ant falls back to earth, and then it dies a meaningless death."

"What happens when we do all of the things involved in the climb to beauty and finally get there?"

The question is followed by thoughtful silence. "The journey up the string," I whisper, "represents one life's opportunity misused."

As a class we sing the chorus of Alabama's hit song, "I'm in a Hurry"—

I'm in a hurry to get things done, oh I

Rush and rush until life's no fun

All I really gotta do is live and die

But I'm in a hurry and don't know why

"If our life seems continually rushed, it offers little enjoyment, and we don't know why," I conclude; "we may be like ants making a difficult climb along a string that robs us of *our life's opportunities* without leading anywhere."

A Word about the Ethical Life

In our modern society, the pursuit of pleasure, status, attractiveness, and wealth have been normalized as the most appropriate means for achieving happiness. In the analogy of *The Ants and the Balloon*, they are like the counterfeit honey that floats high above us. We are considered abnormal if we are not competing with all the other ants to climb the long and tedious string that leads up to them. Yet the string itself represents little more than a lifetime filled with trivial and mundane efforts to get at the things in the balloon. We rush and rush, we're always in a hurry—and we don't even know why. In the end, even if we are able to get our jaws around the things in the balloon, we find that they have no real substance. We fall back to the earth confused as to why our capture of the balloon did not equate with permanent ecstasy.

The paths recommended by the *Aesthetic Life* and the *Ethical Life* are strikingly similar as expressed in our culture. The only difference is that the former is compelled by the desire to gratify biological urges, while the latter results from the desire to conform to social expectations. In both cases, the result is often selfish *pleasure-seeking*. Interestingly, Kierkegaard indicates that the *Ethical Life*, as with the *Aesthetic Life*, will end in despair. But in this case, the despair is not the result of boredom and lack of personal identity; it is instead the result of an inability to attain happiness on the basis of one's own efforts. No matter how diligently we climb the strings, and no matter how many balloons we reach, the strength of our own arm is insufficient to attain salvation.

SPIRITUAL SOLUTIONS

The scriptures explain that we are incapable of reaching happiness or attaining salvation by ourselves—which is the underlying fallacy of the *Ethical Life*. For example, when left to their own strength, the Nephites in the Book of Mormon lost their battles, depleted their prosperity, disrupted their families, and lost their peace and happiness. But when they expressed faith by relying on the strength of the Lord, the opposite result was obtained. In relation to this principle, Nephi said, "O Lord, I have trusted in thee and I will trust in thee forever. I will not put my trust in the arm of the flesh; for I know that cursed is he that putteth his trust in the arm of flesh. Yea cursed is he that putteth his trust in man or maketh flesh his arm" (2 Nephi 4:34). When we seek beauty, or the other things in the balloon, as a means of exalting ourselves or as a means of obtaining happiness, we place our trust in man and expose ourselves to severe consequences.

The scriptures also explain the dangers of pursuing socially defined pleasures as a path to happiness. "He that loveth pleasure shall be a poor man" (Proverbs 21:17). Even if you obtain the balloon, you flutter back to the earth impoverished and empty handed—with nothing of real worth to show for the effort. "She that liveth in pleasure is dead while she liveth" (1 Timothy 5:6). Life on the string drains us of energy and leaves us as though we were dead. "And that which fell among thorns are they, which, when they have heard, go forth and are choked with cares and riches and pleasures of this life, and bring no fruit to perfection" (Luke 8:1–4). Our obsessive care with obtaining the things in the balloon chokes our opportunity for bringing to perfection our true spiritual gifts. "This know also, that in the last days perilous times shall come. For men shall be lovers of pleasures more than lovers of God. From such turn away" (2 Timothy 3:1–5). We truly live in perilous times—for ours is a society of pleasure lovers.

The next chapter reveals some of the conspirators, or lovers of pleasure, that would intentionally send us on a false errand in the pursuit of happiness.

SUMMARY

The *Ethical Life* is defined in terms of conformity to social norms and cultural traditions, and it is carried out at the mind level (thinking as society thinks). It is more pervasive than we realize, and it may ultimately control our behavior. Like genetically controlled sensations of pleasure, social norms and cultural traditions may not be devised for the purpose of maximizing individual happiness. The forces that shape norms and traditions often have other ends in mind.

American social norms and cultural traditions explicitly promote the achievement of beauty, wealth, fame, possessions, and status as the way to realize happiness. As such, it is a destination-oriented philosophy—"you'll be happy when you get there." The targets in this balloon of happiness are external, self-serving, temporary, and often play upon a desire to enhance ease, convenience, sensual pleasure, and personal glory.

The string represents the ladder we must climb to reach the balloon. It represents all of the boredom, hassle, pain, emptiness, drudgery, stress, missed opportunities, and social gamesmanship that accompany the meaningless and mundane ascent to social status. The *Ethical Life* and the *Aesthetic Life* tend to merge in many respects in American culture as conforming to our social norms (the ethical life) has become synonymous with the pursuit of sensual pleasure (the aesthetic life).

The items in the balloon of happiness are not good or bad in and of themselves (for example, education). It is the approach one takes for obtaining them, and the purpose for which they are sought, that determines their worth. If they are pursued as a form of self-gratification with the expectation they will confer lasting happiness of themselves, the result will always be failure. Trying to obtain happiness on our own terms, with socially defined pleasures as the goal, will lead us surely down the same path that ultimately destroyed the Nephite civilization.

CHAPTER TWELVE

DON'T AIM
AT HAPPINESS

———————————————

*There are men in our midst who are trying to build up
themselves at our expense.*
—Joseph Smith

In the preface of *Man's Search for Meaning,* the author Victor Frankl extends a caution: "Don't aim at happiness," he says; "the more you aim at it and make it a target, the more you are going to miss it. For happiness cannot be pursued, it must ensue—as the unintended side effect of one's personal dedication to a course greater than oneself."[1] And yet there are *men in our midst* who point to bright yellow balloons in the sky, as if these were indeed the very targets of happiness, and then herd us onto the strings before we can question why or offer resistance. Who are these balloon masters that prevent us from comprehending that our lives may actually represent some higher cause than seeking happiness from the *golden orbs of honey* to which they direct us?

THE ATTRACTIVENESS BALLOON

"Since it holds so much enticement for so many," I suggest, "let us consider the attribute of 'physical attractiveness' as it floats high above us in a balloon all its own. We already know that there is a biological predisposition for wanting to feel attractive and that there is a genetically controlled sensation of pleasure that rewards successful compliance (that is, it feels good to look good). But how did the social norms and cultural traditions surrounding the attributes of beauty fall into place? Who is the nameless 'they' that created the criteria by which attractiveness is gauged?"

Several opinions erupt from class members who want to finger a culprit. "Men," some say. "Women," counter others, as if the definition of attractiveness were a battlefield, continually fought over by the respective armies of gender. "The fashion industry—the diet/fitness industry—the tobacco industry—the medical industry—male chauvinist pigs." All are proposed as possible explanations.

Blinded by Science

"I'm sorry, but you have it all wrong," Sarah cautions the class. "Listen to what it says in one of my sociology textbooks: 'Research indicates that proportionality is the universal criteria for defining beauty. No matter the overall body size, it is the breast, hip, and waist measurements in relation to one another that define beauty. Inasmuch as proportionality is an accurate indicator of fertility,'" she continues, "'then DNA replication will be enhanced by selecting the mate with the best curves. Genetic programming therefore rewards fertile (attractive) mate selection with a sensation of pleasure. We interpret that pleasure as subjective attraction towards beauty, but it is all biological.'"[2]

Wow, I think to myself, *that was an impressive answer*. The rest of the class is also stunned into silence. After acknowledging the importance of biological factors in influencing definitions of beauty (including the importance of facial symmetry and other theories), I nevertheless argue that it does not entirely account for the wide variation in standards of beauty that have been promoted across different cultures throughout human history.

The Extremes of Beauty

To help clarify this point we make a list of some of the extremes to which the concept of beauty has been taken (few of which have anything to do with breast-hip-waist proportionality or facial symmetry). It does not take long before we have discussed several cultures that either artificially elongate the neck, extensively scar the body, stretch out the lower lips with large plates, or bind the feet to make them smaller. The students recoil in disgust from these disfiguring descriptions.

"Are these the most extreme cases?" I ask innocently. No one seems to be able to think of anything more bizarre, so I offer a few suggestions. "What about cultures that encourage women to have their breasts sliced open so that potentially dangerous bags of silicon can be sewn up inside, or that have their faces cut open so that the fat pads under the cheeks can be removed, or that inject collagen into their lips to make them bigger, or that have openings made in their skin so that large amounts of subcutaneous tissue can be suctioned out, or that have acid poured on their faces to burn off wrinkles, or that . . . "[3]

"All right, already," Carol interrupts. The distaste has now turned inward as our own culture is considered from a new perspective.

A recent article in *USA Today* includes the confession from a TV personality that "I went ahead and got some plastic surgery, like every other good person in America."[4] All of the ants seem to be marching nicely up the string. It seems that few cultures have gone to the extremes that are available to, and even pressed upon, members of our society today. Rather than a bizarre operation, plastic surgery is seen as a normal rite of passage.

I present these issues with the recognition that there may be some among my class who have undergone one or more of the above procedures. But I do it without apology because whether they want me to be or not, I am full of anger on their behalf. I feel that they have been betrayed by their cultural tradition. I am committed to helping them find more productive paths to happiness. And I feel an obligation to help others avoid their mistake—for surely such procedures are a mistake. "There must be very strong forces within our culture," I conclude, "to compel so many women to take such drastic measures to conform to the current, but ever-changing, definition of beauty."

The time had arrived to unmask the villainous Balloon Master that controls the "attractiveness" balloon. Actually, the Balloon Master is a collective of powerful social forces that wields tremendous influence in defining and enforcing images of beauty.

The Fashion Industry

"Why would there be anyone within a society," I ask, "that would want to create a standard for judging beauty? What would they have to gain?"

It takes some time for students to consider the implication of these questions. "Power and control?" Holly suggests.

"How so?" I prompt.

"As we discussed," she continues, "women have genetic programming that compels them to compete with one another on the basis of sexual attractiveness. If you can become the authority and establish the criteria for defining attractiveness—then you control the ability of people to satisfy a biological urge that may be as strong as hunger."

I am impressed with how quickly and fully the students have comprehended the insights we have discussed. "If you want to maximize the amount of power you possess to the fullest extent possible," I continue to question, "how will you define beauty?"

This stumps them for awhile. Then suddenly the light clicks for Brittany. "You would define it very narrowly so that it excludes most women," she concludes. "You would want to make it a scarce commodity." As one who desperately desires to be attractive, she frowns at her own conclusion.

"True," I agree, "but why?"

"For money," she says. "You define it very narrowly, but then you tell all those who are left out that it's OK, because you have a product to sell them (make-up, hairstyles, fashionable clothes, surgical procedures, etc.) that will help mask their deformity."

"The average fashion model," I note "is five to six inches taller than the average woman and yet weighs 24 percent less. Less than five percent of the population naturally fits the body type that the fashion industry promotes. The other 95 percent of the population spends billions of dollars each year trying to fit."[5]

"Besides that," Sarah (plain and tall) comments angrily, "the fashion industry almost exclusively promotes very revealing styles in clothing and swimwear so that those who aren't skinny can be easily identified and shamed into trying harder and buying more products. What we need," she says, "is a more realistic standard of beauty that appreciates us larger types."

"Power, control, *and wealth* go to the group that can establish cultural standards of beauty," I conclude. "While the criteria for beauty will continue to evolve and change with time, beauty will never be defined by our culture in a way that includes more than a fraction of the population. There is too much money and power at stake."

I recall an article in the February 1997 issue of *Psychology Today*. It notes that a high percentage of women are either intimidated by, or angry with, fashion model images because of the narrow and unrealistic (hence, largely unobtainable) image of beauty they portray. Most women, the article concludes, are dying to have a broader image of beauty portrayed—one that includes a variety of female shapes. But it will never happen.[6]

"The fact that the current standard is very thin is not the

problem," I argue with some emotion; "the problem lies in having any standard at all. As long as a standard of any type exists, some people will be hurt and excluded." I sadly conclude that "as long as there is a fashion industry, there will always be a standard, and it will always seek to keep out most women. The attractiveness balloon will always float high in the sky, and too many women will waste the energy of their lives trying to reach it."

A 1999 study found that "in many Developing World communities, being overweight is associated with beauty, prosperity, health, and prestige," while "thinness is perceived to be a sign of ill health or poverty, and is something to be feared and avoided." The study went on to note that "in areas where it is easy to become fat, society's preference is for thinness; conversely in parts of the world where it is easy to remain lean, those societies prefer plumpness."[7] Overall, the desirability for plumpness was found in 81 percent of developing societies.

It is also interesting to note that, as in our culture, "beauty" in other societies is typically grouped together in a balloon that includes such traits as "prosperity" and "prestige."

The Diet/Fitness Industries

While the fashion industry is primarily concerned with maintaining the power to define beauty in an exclusive way, the diet/fitness industry has a vested interest in making sure that the exclusive definition continues to revolve around thinness, fitness, and body weight. Current estimates place the annual gross revenues of the diet industry alone at more than $50 billion dollars.[8]

"What is the cultural message of the diet and fitness industry?" I ask.

"They try to make you feel that to be acceptable in this culture you must be thin and fit," Holly says, "and that to be thin and fit you must use diet and fitness products."

"Sadly, the advertisements for a large number of diet and fitness products depict a scantily clad female torso, from the upper thighs to the chin (no face)," I explain. "Again, what is the cultural message?"

"The only thing that makes females valuable, apparently, is how they look from the thighs to the shoulders," Holly continues with sarcasm and anger, "and the only way to look that way is to buy their products."

It is a powerful message that both supports and feeds off the fashion industry. The collusion becomes even more insidious when the diet and fitness industries try to align themselves with health and medicine.

The Tobacco Industry

It does not take long for one to imagine the goal of the tobacco industry in relation to body size. "What is the message of cigarette ads that target women?" I wonder out loud.

Carol explains, "I've never seen an ad that does not use the words *slim* or *thin* or *sleek,* or something to make you think that you will be skinnier if you smoke their brand. They want you to think that smoking cigarettes is a good way to improve your health by helping you slim down."[9]

"It's unfortunate," observes Sarah, "that the women's movement has been diminished and tarnished by the tobacco industry as they have tried to associate the use of tobacco with increased freedom and sophistication for women."

I agree. It is sad when the tobacco slogan *You've Come a Long Way Baby* can be applied to the fact that tobacco-related lung cancer deaths now take the lives of more women than does breast cancer.[10]

The Gender Perceptions

"I still think it's men that cause the problem by demanding that you look a certain way before they pay any attention to you," Brittany says. "You go to a dance on campus and you can plan on holding up the walls all night unless you are as skinny as a pencil. Now, I think that's the guys' fault."

"I think women are more offended by curves than men," I observe. "Is the reason that you have to be skinny as a pencil to get a dance because men really prefer women to be skinny, or is it because women try to convince men that only women who are as skinny as a pencil are good enough to dance with?" No one is happy about this question.

I point out that research conducted with an assortment of female silhouettes indicates that men prefer fuller figures than women think they do. (Most men in my classes are turned off by the excessively skinny fashion models that predominate in magazines.) Further, most women select a silhouette to identify their own shape that is one or two sizes fuller than reality. So without really knowing what men prefer, women keep thinking they are bigger than they really are and keep trying to get skinnier than men want them to be.

On the other hand, both men and women often view an attractive woman (as defined by society's standards) as a status symbol for a man. I refer to a study to clarify my position. "The picture of a man in a business suit is shown to an auditorium full of people who rate him on a scale of 1 to 10 in order to establish a baseline rating," I explain. "Another audience then rates his picture, but this time there is an attractive woman next to him. A third audience finally rates the man, but there is an unattractive woman in the picture. Even though the picture of the man is identical all three times, what happens to his rating?" I question.

Every class intuitively responds, correctly, that the man's rating goes up with the attractive woman and down with the unattractive woman. "Therefore," I note, "a man who is primarily concerned with his own *status*, one of the rewards in the balloon and one of the benchmarks of *The Ethical Life*, will choose a woman who most closely approximates the current social standard of feminine beauty, regardless of his personal preference."

Most men who have gone through my weight-loss class look at current pictures of fashion models and shake their heads in wonder that such images could be promoted as the highest standard for beauty. Yet, if society keeps telling those same men that skinny women really are more attractive, then they will choose them as dance partners (even if they personally find them less attractive), because they want to enhance their own image. When the *Ethical Life* dominates, women try to become "attractive" as defined by cultural tradition, and men try to enhance their "status" by associating with attractive women. It seems a bit shallow doesn't it?

CONCLUDING POSTSCRIPT ABOUT THE BALLOON MASTER

"No matter whose pernicious efforts are at the core," I say, "the Masters of the Beauty Balloon have been very successful in making the balloon very desirable as a goal for happiness and in excluding the majority of people from obtaining it. The February 1997 issue of *Psychology Today* released the results of a poll that attempted to ascertain levels of body satisfaction. Not surprisingly, the levels of dissatisfaction were higher than ever before, and the percentage of those dissatisfied was rising faster than ever. People have never had a greater desire to be attractive, and yet they have never felt so far from hitting the mark. The Balloon Masters are masters indeed."[11]

SPIRITUAL SOLUTIONS

How much more at risk for error are we as we wander adrift in a society whose traditions are all secular? We are surrounded by "Balloon Masters" who have nothing at heart but their own profit. Their sole intent is to provoke feelings of inferiority that will compel us to buy the products that they pander. They teach us to chase their balloons, and in so doing we lose our souls. The scriptures continually warn us about the dangers of following the traditions of men, rather than the teachings of the Savior. "Why do ye also transgress the commandment of God by your tradition?" (Matthew 15:3).

King Benjamin identifies the key for overcoming false social customs. "I say unto you, my sons, were it not for these things, which have been kept and preserved by the hand of God, that we might read and understand of his mysteries, and have his commandments always before our eyes, that even our fathers would have dwindled in unbelief, and we should have been like unto our brethren, the Lamanites, who know nothing concerning these things, or even do not believe them when they are taught them, because of the traditions of their fathers, which are not correct" (Mosiah 1:5). It is by studying the scriptures and following the teachings of the prophets that we are able to discern false traditions, so that we might be "kept and preserved by the hand of God."

Just as Tevya rose above the temptations of the *Ethical Life* by choosing faith before secular conformity, it is time for us to pop the balloons of our secular culture and consider a deeper *Spiritual Life* as promoted by Kierkegaard. As Victor Frankl warned, we must avoid the tendency to "aim at happiness," like a balloon in the sky. Instead we must let happiness "ensue—as the unintended side effect of one's personal dedication to a course greater than oneself."

SUMMARY

Social definitions for beauty vary across time and culture. Beauty standards prey upon the biologically programmed desire to be attractive but are created within societies for the purpose of consolidating power, control, and wealth among those who define and enforce the standard. In the United States, the fashion industry maintains power by creating a standard of beauty that excludes most women. The current standard of thinness is then exploited by the diet/fitness, medical, and tobacco industries to promote products and enhance profits (not happiness).

When the *Ethical Life* dominates, women try to enhance personal well-being by conforming to culturally defined standards of attractiveness. At the same time, men try to enhance their social status by associating with "attractive" women (those who conform best). This creates a vicious cycle where the competition to be most attractive leads to more extreme definitions of beauty and higher levels of body dissatisfaction.

While it is hard to feel sorry for them, men who want to enhance their prestige choose to associate with women who increasingly deviate from their preferences. As long as we judge the value of ourselves and others in light of the prevailing social norms and cultural traditions, *we* are the problem. We are the ants on the string who put pressure on those around us to keep climbing.

While the social forces that define beauty are powerful, and even though the biological need to feel attractive is very strong, we have a choice to base the motivation for our behavior at a level that is higher than the body or the mind. In addition to the *Aesthetic Life* and the *Ethical Life*, Kierkegaard also described the *Spiritual Life*. While it is difficult to follow the *Spiritual Life* in a society that almost exclusively emphasizes the pursuit of happiness at the mind and body levels, there is hope.

SECTION V

THE SPIRIT AND
SELF-ACTUALIZATION

The Greek term for happiness, *eudaimonia*, captures the underlying process of self-actualization. *Eudaimonia* is defined as the "actualization of a soul with respect to its proper function." Interestingly, in Greek philosophy the realization of happiness is conditional upon the attainment of self-actualization. The summit of Maslow's hierarchy must be reached, and all of the foundational needs met (love and acceptance, self-esteem), before the deepest levels of satisfaction and happiness can be experienced.

The Greek position argues that the proper function of a soul, or *eudaimonia*, can be realized only if the spirit, or inner genius, is the guide. But the appetites of the body, and the pressures of social conformity, continually attempt to usurp leadership of the soul and thereby undermine the process of self-actualization. This section takes an in-depth look at the motivation, nature, and true role of the body, mind, and spirit and offers guidelines for uniting these three forces in the pursuit of a higher purpose. If successful, the process of self-actualization goes forward and the image in the mirror becomes a valued partner, rather than a scorned enemy.

CHAPTER THIRTEEN

THE PURPOSE OF LIFE

*A man filled with the love of God is not content with blessing his family
alone, but ranges through the whole world, anxious to
bless the whole human race.*
—Joseph Smith

I have an antique sword mounted in my office as a physical reminder of a man who had the courage to live the *Spiritual Life* to the highest degree. Today, I reverently take it down, place a worn and rusty helmet upon my head, and with a broken shield at my side stand boldly before the class. After taking a deep breath and fixing my gaze upon some imagined star, I begin a new session of class: "I shall impersonate a man: his name, Alonzo Quixana, a country gentleman, no longer young. Being retired he has much time for books. He studies them from morn till night, and often through the night till morn again. And all he reads oppresses him, fills him with indignation at man's murderous ways towards man. He ponders the question—how to make better a world, where evil brings profit and virtue brings none at all? But fraud, deceit, and malice are mingled with truth and sincerity. He broods and broods and broods and broods and broods, and finally his brains dry up. He lays down the melancholy burden of sanity and conceives the strangest project ever imagined—to become a knight errant and sally forth to roam the world in search of adventures, to right all wrongs, to mount a crusade to raise up the weak and those in need. After his preparations are complete, he seizes his sword.

No longer will he remain Alonzo Quixana, but a dauntless knight known as Don Quixote de la Mancha."

Even though I pronounce this last line with much energy and conviction, I sense that my charade has only bewildered the students. Undaunted, I lay aside the armor and ask a question that is admittedly ambiguous. "So, what is the purpose of life?" I hope for a comment that relates to Alonzo Quixana's transformation, or his commitment to mount a noble crusade, or his desire to raise up the weak and those in need, but my expectations are met with silence.

"Fine," I say, increasingly irritated with the seemingly lifeless bodies assembled before me, "I would now like you to get into small groups of three or four and share with one another the *purpose of your* life." I am forced to yell, "*Now*," rather sharply in order to elicit any movement. A glint of light from my drawn sword provides further incentive. Even then, the assignment is accomplished only with the aid of groans, murmurs, and audible sighs.

Once the laborious process of assembling them into groups is finished, many still rely on eye rolling, folded arms, and tightly pursed lips to see them through the painful formality of introductions. Finally, someone in the group actually starts to share feelings. After a few minutes, other students become more involved, and after ten minutes—when I am telling them to disassemble their groups—many are begging for more time.

"How did you rate or judge other people when you first came into this class room?" I ask once they back in their original seats.

Eventually Brittany says, "Mostly by how they looked, or what they were wearing."

"In other words," I offer, "you initially judged each other on appearance (prompted by the need to compete on the basis of attractiveness) and by what people were wearing (a sign of social status). In short, you evaluated each other almost exclusively at the body (*Aesthetic*) and mind (*Ethical*) levels."

"I guess," Brittany concedes grudgingly.

"How did you evaluate each other after being in groups together?" I continue.

They think for awhile before Sarah finally answers. "It wasn't really 'judging' each other on the basis of *differences*, like before, as much as it was appreciating all of the unexpected *similarities*. We found out that many of our dreams were alike and that we wanted many of the same things out of life. The purpose represented by our lives was comparable in many ways."

"What happened to the importance of the initial judgments after you had found some common ground in relation to the vision that each of you has for your life?"

"They didn't seem to matter so much anymore," explains Kristen. "In fact, I completely forgot about how people looked or what they were wearing after I got to know them at a different level."

"Interacting at that 'different level,'" I explain, "is what Kierkegaard meant by the *Spiritual Life*. Further," I say, taking up my sword, "it was the call of the *Spiritual Life* that animated the worthy deeds of the dauntless knight, Don Quixote de la Mancha."

THE VOID IN OUR HEARTS

The pursuit of happiness at the body level (the *Aesthetic Life*) is motivated by the desire to obtain genetically controlled sensual pleasure. Instead, the path ends in such boredom and despair that it compels one to the extremity of addiction and obsession. The pursuit of happiness at the mind level (the *Ethical Life*) is motivated by the desire to earn praise by exemplifying social norms and cultural traditions. Pointless and dreary efforts to obtain the prizes that society dangles before us are rewarded with short-lived feelings of self-importance that soon turn to emptiness and frustration. How then, can we fill the void in our hearts?—the void that when filled we equate with happiness.

Kierkegaard asks us to bravely confront the void in our hearts that cannot be filled by "aesthetic" pleasures or "ethical" rules. He asks us to conquer the void, to put it to rout, to throw it down and be free of its power forever. He asks us to live the *Spiritual Life* and to fill the void in our hearts with three things—love and acceptance, purpose and meaning, and self-expression. It is time to take him at his word.

"Consider our brave knight, Don Quixote," I continue passionately, strapping on my gear and taking up the sword. "He arrives at a broken-down inn (but to him a lofty castle). After several misadventures, he begs a boon of the innkeeper—or rather, the Lord of the Castle. Realizing that he has not yet been knighted, he asks that very favor of the Lord, who is willing to grant the favor if the ill-fated knight will but leave his castle (and thereby put an end to the chaos that continually surrounds him). An agreement reached, Don Quixote spends the night fasting and holding vigil in the courtyard." I assume the character of Don Quixote and give voice to the imaginations that surround his pending coronation: "Now I must consider how sages of the future will describe this historic night. 'Long after the sun had retired to his couch, darkening the gates and balconies of La Mancha, Don Quixote, with lofty expression and measured tread, held vigil in the courtyard of a mighty mansion . . . '

"Oh thou maker of empty boasts. On this of all nights to give way to vanity. No! Don Quixote, take a deep breath of life and consider how it should be lived. Call nothing thine, except thy soul. Love not what thou art, but only what thou may become. Do not pursue pleasure, for thou mayest have the misfortune to overtake it. Look always forward, in last year's nest there are no birds this year. Be just to all men, courteous to all women. I come in a world of iron to make a world of gold."

After this speech, the class and I sing together the song *To Dream the Impossible Dream*.

"As he holds vigil in the courtyard," I ask at the conclusion of our song, "what is the struggle that takes place in the heart of our worthy knight, and what is the outcome?"

By now most of the students are involved and interested. "At first he is tempted to follow the *Ethical Life* by seeking fame and glory," Carol says, "but then he kind of humbles himself and commits himself to a higher purpose or a spiritual quest—'I come in a world of iron to make a world of gold.'"

"He also pledges to avoid the *Aesthetic Life* by not pursuing pleasure," Kristen comments. "Unlike Tevya, who dreams of wealth as the solution to his desire for happiness, Don Quixote seems to understand that to overtake pleasure may be a misfortune, rather than a source of happiness."

Excellent answers, I think to myself. But what are the elements of his *Spiritual Life?* How will he fill the void that is in his heart, if not with pleasure or vanity?

THE PHILOSOPHY OF EUDAIMONISM

To answer this question, an ancient Greek philosophy called *eudaimonism* is introduced to the class. The root word is *d-a-i-m-o-n*. It is Greek for "genius" or "spirit." Further, the prefix "eu-" means "good" or "well." And the suffix "-ism" refers to a "doctrine" or "theory." As such, *eudaimonism* means the doctrine of the good spirit, or more accurately, the theory of the realized genius. The Greek term *eudaimonia* is often translated into English using the word "happiness." As such, this philosophy has intriguing implications for the pursuit of happiness.[1]

The doctrine is meant as a philosophy, or a way of thinking, about the realization of personal well-being. It offers a well-marked path in relation to Aristotle's observation that "more than anything else men and women seek happiness." In short, it represents the pattern for Kierkegaard's concept of the *Spiritual Life*, and it is epitomized by the life of Don Quixote.

The philosophy of *eudaimonism* has *three maxims* that serve to define the path to self-actualization. Almost all philosophical, psychological, and spiritual traditions emphasize the primary importance of self-awareness or self-understanding. The Greeks, however, summed up the concept most concisely, and expressed it most poetically, in the *first maxim* of *eudaimonism*—'know thyself.'

KNOW THYSELF

The underlying assumption of *eudaimonism* is that each individual has within her or him a *daimon*—an inner spirit or genius of infinite value that is unique to them. If the genius goes unrealized, then it is forever lost to the world, and the joy of all humanity is diminished—for no other person will be able to make the exact same contribution of spirit and genius.

At this point, I cannot keep from kneeling in the middle of the classroom and saying to the students, "I have a little secret for you. Huddle up. Huddle up." Unlike the students of John Keating, as played by Robin Williams in *Dead Poet's Society*, my students never do huddle up. I am left all alone, kneeling on the floor, feeling somewhat silly. Even so, I continue: "We don't read and write poetry because it's cute. We read and write poetry because we are members of the human race, and the human race is filled with passion. Now, medicine, law, business, engineering, these are noble pursuits and necessary to sustain life, but poetry, beauty, romance, love—these are what we stay alive for. To quote from Whitman, 'O me, O life, of the questions of these recurring, of the endless lines of the faithless, of the cities filled with the foolish, what good amid all these, O me, O life.' Answer: That you are here, that life exists, an identity, that the powerful play goes on, and you may contribute a verse. What will your verse be?"

I rise from my awkward position on the floor. "First of all," I explain, "you must believe with all your heart, just like the ancient Greeks, that you have a beautiful, worthwhile verse to contribute to the play of life (or a *daimon* to realize). Then, to satisfy the first maxim, you must devote all of your energies to the search for that verse. It may take a lifetime to fully discover, but it's there, inside of you. Just as Don Quixote urged himself, we must all 'take a deep breath of life and consider how it should be lived.'"

"But how can we find out 'who we are'?" Sarah wonders out loud.

"Good question," I answer. "How can we?"

Exposure to Ideas

This question gives the class a chance to mull over the importance of self-discovery and to discuss different strategies for trying to enhance it. Eventually several appropriate insights come forth from different students. "Earnest study in a variety of disciplines helps people find out who they are and where they stand on different issues," offers Carol. "That's why I decided to go back to school. As I am exposed to different ideas in textbooks and classes, it clarifies my thinking about who *I* am and what *I* think is important in life."

Research has demonstrated that as individuals become more preoccupied with obtaining wealth, one of the balloons of the ethical life, the less energy they devote to a personal philosophy of life, and the less they consider "how it should be lived."[2] We all have a need to step back from our busy lives and search out the great ideas in the best books of the world. It was by reading his books "from morn till night, and often through the night till morn again" that Don Quixote discovered his true calling in the form knight errantry.

Introspection

"I think introspection is important," Holly says. "Things like prayer, meditation, and mental imagery are helpful in understanding who we are. Not very many people take time to just be with themselves."

It is interesting to compare and contrast some Eastern philosophies with those of the West in relation to the importance of personal introspection. The great traditions of Eastern meditation, for example, stress the primary importance of enhancing self-understanding, while the secular traditions of the West deal with the imperative of seeking material gain. But in the process, we may miss the opportunity to just be with our own thoughts—through prayer, meditation, and pondering—to the point that we never come to discover who we really are. Again, it was introspection that allowed Don Quixote to ask the question that would chart his future course; "he *ponders* the question—how to make better a world . . ."

But it will be much less effective, if not counterproductive, if we seek insight through meditation, prayer, and introspection without seeking heavenly guidance as part of that process. Kierkegaard suggested that ultimately it is through faith in God that one discovers his unique and eternal vocation. In fact, he declared that an attempt to develop as an individual without recognizing that inner potential is a gift from God, and without relying upon God to guide personal development, is the sin of defiance. Our *eudaimonistic* development will be firm if we follow the counsel to "trust in the Lord with all thine heart; and lean not unto thine own understanding. In all thy ways acknowledge him, and he shall direct thy paths" (Proverbs 3:5–6).

Personal Experience

"Experiencing life as fully as possible," Matthew says, "and trying to understand what different experiences mean, is the most important thing. Based on the positive and negative experiences, we come more clearly to understand our strengths and weaknesses. Self-awareness requires that we be participants in life, rather than spectators." It is the first comment Matthew has ever made in this class that has not compelled his fellow students to roll their eyes.

As our society increasingly relies on vicarious experience obtained by watching other peoples' lives on television or in the media, we lose the understanding about ourselves that we might obtain if it were instead *our* sleeves that were rolled up and *our* sweat running down our faces. While there are a finite number of experiences that we can engage in, exposing ourselves to new ideas, and engaging in sincere introspection, can lead us to those experiences that will allow us to understand and help define who we are. At that point, we too will be compelled to take up our sword and "sally forth to roam the world in search of adventures."

"When we discover our passions through study, introspection, and fully participating in life," I agree with the students, "then we are getting very close to understanding our *daimon* and knowing where our passions lie."

BECOME WHO YOU ARE

As we begin to gain insights into the nature of our *daimon*, and thereby begin to satisfy the demands of the first maxim, then we are challenged to find ways to *follow* the promptings of that inner *daimon*. As mentioned earlier, one translation of *daimon* is genius. It is, therefore, interesting to consider the use of that word by Henry David Thoreau: "If one listens to the faintest, but constant, suggestions of his genius, which are certainly true, he sees not to what extremes, or even insanity, it may lead him; and yet that way, as he grows more resolute and faithful, his road lies."[3]

Since our *daimon* represents 'who we are,' then following the promptings of our *daimon*, or inner genius, will allow us to *become who we are*. This is the *second maxim* of *eudaimonism*. Henry David

Thoreau continues: "No man ever followed his genius till it misled him. Though the result were bodily weakness, yet perhaps no one can say that the consequences were to be regretted, for these were a life in conformity to higher principles."[4] Life in conformity to higher principles suggests a nobler inspiration for behavior than pleasure-seeking or social conformity. As Henry David Thoreau points out, however, following our *daimon* and striving to become who we are may lead to certain extremes, bodily weakness, and even insanity.

"Insanity," I whisper, more to myself than to my students, "Insanity." Once again, I fit myself with the armor of The Knight.

"The spiritual quest of Don Quixote led him to extremes, bodily weakness, and even insanity. Insanity, at least, as defined by others. The family and friends of Don Quixote," I explain somewhat heatedly, "were fearful that his 'insanity' would reflect poorly on them. They were staunch practitioners of the *Ethical Life*, and, as such, were far more concerned about their good image and their chances for inheriting Don Quixote's wealth, than they were concerned for the tired knight's spiritual well-being. At last they were successful in breaking both his delusion of knighthood and his spirit. The result was his death."

Imitating Miguel de Cervantes, the creator of Don Quixote, as quoted in the musical *Man of La Mancha* I ask the class passionately, "When life itself seems lunatic, who knows where madness lies? Perhaps to be too practical is madness. To surrender dreams, this may be madness—to seek treasure where there is only trash. Too much sanity may be madness. And maddest of all, to see life as it is—not as it should be."

I then reflect, "To surrender the path that is illuminated by our *daimon*, to seek treasure in the emptiness of pretty balloons—this may be true madness. When the sincere pursuit of our *daimon* takes us in a direction that runs counter to social norms and cultural traditions, then we are at best labeled as 'different,' and at worst as 'insane'—and 'yet that way, as [we] grow more resolute and faithful, [our] road lies. For these [are] a life in conformity to higher principles.'"

At this point, I am compelled to consider another scene from *Dead Poet's Society*. Mr. Keating has asked the boys to walk around the courtyard. Before long they are marching in time to a military cadence. After instructing them about the dangers of blind conformity to custom, tradition, and peer pressure, John Keating passionately says to them: "Now we all have a great need of acceptance. But you must trust that your beliefs are unique, your own. Even though others may think them odd or unpopular. Even though the crowd may go— 'That's Baaaaad.' Robert Frost said, 'Two roads diverged in the wood, and I, I took the one less traveled by, and that has made all the difference.'"

Trying to match the passion of Mr. Keating, I explain that "the road less traveled is the one that is revealed by the inner 'suggestions of . . . genius, which are certainly true.' The road less traveled is the path of personal happiness. We are faced with a choice, either to become who we are (the realization of our inner genius), or to become what we do (a wasted soul whose energy gets lost while climbing a futile string). We can diligently strive to fight against the current and follow the whisperings within us to become who we are, or we can allow the unguided twists and turns of life and the roles that we fill by chance to ultimately define us."

SHARE WHO YOU ARE WITH OTHERS

"And for what purpose shall we *become who we are?*" I ask the class rhetorically. "Why shall we follow the road less traveled? To enhance our own glory and fame? To increase our material wealth? To win the praise of society?" These questions are followed by a pause, and then a quiet and thoughtful response.

"No," explains Sarah. "We should become who we are so that we can be more useful in the task of turning a 'world of iron into a world of gold.'"

"What is it about becoming who we are," I persist, "that will bring happiness?"

"Happiness, true happiness, joy," she explains more precisely, "can be fully experienced only by first striving to understand and realize our inner potential and then by applying our developing genius, or *daimon*, towards the process of making the world a better place. To be happy," she says emphatically, "we must become who we are so that we can share who we are with others."

"This," I say, admiring her depth of understanding, "is the *third maxim of eudaimonism—to share who you are with others*. Just as Don Quixote first developed and then exercised the strength of his good right arm on behalf of 'the weak and those in need,' it must also be our quest to find and strengthen our abilities that we might be worthy and capable of serving one another. Such a course is required," I conclude, "to experience a life of joy."

I ask the students to comment on the vision or dream for their life that they shared with each other as the class began. Many express their hopes and ambitions with passion, and with a fuller understanding of how they relate to the philosophy of *eudaimonism*. After listing their dreams on the board, we are able to conclude that at the core, most represent the desire to (a) *first realize personal potential* and to then (b) *be a force for good in the lives of others*. These two themes are so consistent among my students that they seem to represent universal, spiritual desires. It is too bad, I think to myself, that there are so many barriers that get in the way.

A DAIMON OR A ROLE

At the same time, many dreams that were listed on the board are defined by family, church, and career *roles*. I want to be a good "mother," "member of my church," or "teacher" are common responses.

"What is the potential danger of defining our life's purpose in terms of a role?" I ask.

"Roles can all be taken away?" Holly replies tentatively.

"True," I agree, "and what if we have defined our lives in terms of the role that is lost?"

"The importance of our life is diminished," she continues. "We run the risk of withdrawing from society and thinking that our ability to contribute is over."

"How can we avoid this risk?" I continue to probe.

The students fail to think of an alternative. "Perhaps," I offer in support, "our higher purpose or quest should be broad enough to unite and give direction to each of the roles we occupy. Even if all of our roles are lost, the dream would still be there to guide us. Don Quixote's 'roles' were all taken away, but his all-encompassing quest 'to raise up the weak and those in need' was never lost. Instead it served to guide all of his interactions at every level."

Thinking of my own life, I decide that since my students had shared openly, it would be an appropriate gesture on my part to return that trust. "My dream, as it exists now," I say tentatively, "is to gain insight and understanding, and to then share that insight and understanding in a way that helps other people more fully realize their dreams." I am encouraged by the fact that no one snickers. Sarah comments that my vision is also based on the same two themes that were identified in the goals expressed by most of the students.

"In short," I conclude, after confessing my many shortcomings in relation to this calling, "My dream is to be a teacher—not as a career necessarily, although that is what I do for a living—but as a creed for conducting my life in general. This cause motivates my interactions and involvement with my family members, my church, my community, and my profession. I think about it constantly, and it infuses each role I have with enthusiasm and meaning. But of itself," I emphasize, "it is not a role. No matter what happens to me, or what roles are eventually taken away from me, that quest will still exist. It represents the purpose of my life."

SPIRITUAL SOLUTIONS

In his teachings, President Gordon B. Hinckley regularly expresses sentiments that are consistent with the three maxims of *eudaimonism*. But his teachings go beyond the philosophies of men, for they are infused with knowledge and understanding that is available only to a prophet of God. In relation to the maxim, *Know Thyself*, President Hinckley says: "There is something of divinity within each of you. You have such tremendous potential with that light as part of your inherited nature."[5] The ability to grasp this truth in relation to our divine nature is central to spiritual growth and development, and to the experience of happiness.

In relation to the second maxim, *Become Who You Are*, President Hinckley continues: "Everyone of you was endowed by your Father in Heaven with a tremendous capacity to do good in the world. Train your minds and your hands that you many be equipped to serve the society of which you are a member."[6] Training our minds and hearts is the goal of becoming who we are.

In relation to the third maxim, *Share Who You Are with Others*, President Hinckley concludes by saying: "Cultivate the art of being kind, of being thoughtful, of being helpful. Build within you the quality of mercy which comes as a part of the divine attributes you have inherited."[7] Kindness, thoughtfulness, mercy, and being helpful are the appropriate outward expressions of those who have comprehended their true nature and who have worked to develop their divine talents.

It is by discovering, developing, and using our divine abilities to

THE PURPOSE OF LIFE

comfort and raise others that we at last experience the type of "happiness" that is intended by the word *eudaimonia*—"the actualization of a soul with respect to its proper function." This is also the meaning for the concept of "joy," *the true purpose of life*. For "men are that they might have joy" (2 Nephi 2:25).

SUMMARY

In our first interaction with others, we typically focus on the differences over which we compete (attractiveness, clothes, and so on). Thus we are isolated by our desire to measure up or to outdo each other. This interaction occurs at the body (*aesthetic*) or mind (*ethical*) level and leaves us with an emptiness or void in our hearts. Once we come to know others based on the quality of their life purpose (the dream or vision that they have for their life), our focus is on our similarities (*spiritual* level). Physical and social differences lose their meaning and go largely unnoticed.

The philosophy of *eudaimonism* offers insight as to how we can avoid the temptations of the *aesthetic* and *ethical lives* and how the *Spiritual Life* might actually be lived. This philosophy also becomes the path to filling the void in our hearts and realizing happiness. The underlying premise of *eudaimonism* is that each person is endowed with a unique genius that is of great worth. We must believe with all our hearts, just as the ancient Greeks, that we each have a beautiful, worthwhile verse to contribute to the play of life.

The first maxim of *eudaimonism*, to *know thyself*, requires the devotion of time and energy in the form of introspection, personal study, and meaningful experience so that we might better understand the nature of our inherent genius, or spiritual gift. The second maxim, to *become who you are*, requires a lifetime of training to develop the skills and abilities that are unique to us.

The third maxim, to *share who you are with others*, suggests that the true worth of our abilities is not realized unless they are applied toward the benefit of our fellow creatures. Too often, we try to narrowly define the purpose of our lives in terms of family, career, or other specific roles. The true quest of our lives should be defined in terms that transcend any one role, but that animate each of our roles with passion and meaning.

As we follow the light of our emerging genius, we will never be led astray—even if others condemn, ridicule, or attempt to thwart our efforts. It is by understanding, developing, and using our divine abilities to comfort and raise others that we at last throw off the *aesthetic* and *ethical lives* and experience the true happiness and joy that can come only from the *Spiritual Life*.

CHAPTER FOURTEEN

A MIGHTY CHANGE
OF HEART

I believe in the principle that I can make a difference in this world.
—Gordon B. Hinckley

The greatest regret of Jacob Marley's ghost was that during his lifetime his preoccupation with wealth caused him to miss opportunities to make a difference in the world, especially in the lives of his fellow creatures. "Why did I walk through crowds of fellow-beings with my eyes turned down," he laments, "and never raise them to that blessed Star which led the Wise Men to a poor abode! Were there no poor homes to which its light would have conducted me!"[1]

We begin this session of class by reviewing and clarifying the *motivation*, *nature*, and true *role* of the body, mind, and spirit, as they relate to the pursuit of happiness. In the end, it all revolves around the feeling that our individual lives can make a difference, the feeling that we can contribute a meaningful verse to the play of life and that others might benefit as a result. For many of us, to obtain this feeling will require a profound change of heart.

THE TRUE ROLE OF THE SPIRIT

Our spiritual *nature* is derived from our relationship with our Heavenly Father. As his spiritual children we have inherited his qualities and potential. It is this divine nature that animates the unique spiritual gifts and talents that we possess. As the offspring of deity, our spiritual *nature* is endowed with all of the attributes necessary for future development into Godhood. As Gordon B. Hinckley observed, "There is a mighty strength that comes of the knowledge that you and I are the sons and daughters of God. Within us is something of the divine."[2]

In the pursuit of happiness, the natural *motivation* of the spirit is to search for meaning, meet the need to express love and acceptance, and satisfy the desire to develop and share spiritual gifts. In reference to expressing love, Joseph Smith Jr. said that "love is one of the chief characteristics of Deity, and ought to be manifested by those who aspire to become sons of God."[3] All of the higher needs in Maslow's hierarchy (self-esteem, love and acceptance, self-actualization) are in truth spiritual needs that can only be fulfilled through spiritual growth and development.

The *role* of the spirit is to coordinate and guide the activities of the body and mind toward the magnification of spiritual talents, and toward the realization of divine destiny. The spirit must be the guiding force if the result is to be spiritual growth and development and, ultimately, happiness—previously defined as "the actualization of a soul with respect to its proper function." It is only when the appetites of the body and the social pressures of the mind are subdued by the influence of the spirit that we can discover our inner genius— allowing us to take in hand the symbolic sword with which we can blaze the path of our destined crusade. It is the body, mind, and spirit—when united toward a common purpose—that propel the *soul* along a course of *proper function* to the ultimate realization of happiness.

THE TRUE ROLE OF THE BODY

At its most fundamental level, the *nature* of the body can be described in terms of a highly complex biological organism that has developed as an efficient mechanism for enhancing the ability of

DNA to replicate successfully. All living organisms, including our bodies, are simply the equipment that DNA employs to further its ceaseless work of replication.

In the pursuit of happiness, the biological *motivation* (or negative temptation) of the body is to respond to genetic programming that rewards survival-enhancing behaviors with pleasure. If one pursues happiness at the body level, then it will be sought by maximizing physical sensations of pleasure. The strength of biological urges to engage in certain behaviors is very great, and the levels of corresponding pleasure are very high. But it is in reference to such biologically driven pleasure-seeking that the scriptures refer to the "natural man" as an "enemy to God" (Mosiah 3:19).

In contrast, the true spiritual *role* of the body is to serve as the physical home of the spirit and to serve the purpose of its higher development. "Know ye not," Paul exclaimed, "that ye are the temple of God, and that the spirit of God dwelleth in you?" (1 Corinthians 3:16). Paul further explains that this special relationship between the body and spirit requires us to surrender ownership of our bodies for the higher cause of serving the needs of the spirit. "Your body is the temple of the Holy Ghost which is in you, which ye have of God, and ye are not your own" (1 Corinthians 6:19). The Book of Mormon is even more explicit in explaining that "the natural man is an enemy to God . . . unless he yields to the enticings of the Holy Spirit" (Mosiah 3:19).

From a spiritual perspective, the physical body provides the spirit with sensory input, allowing the spirit to perceive and comprehend the beauty of God's creations. At the same time, the body serves as an outlet of spiritual expression in the form of music, movement, art and other activities. But in all things, the *spirit* must be the guide, and the *role* of the body is to yield to the leadership or "enticings of the Holy Spirit." Most physical pleasures have a proper place and time, but only as prescribed by the spirit. As such, this is not a doctrine of utter self-denial, but a doctrine of moderation and balance that recognizes the necessity of superseding biological compulsions with spiritual guidance.

THE TRUE ROLE OF THE MIND

The *nature* of the mind is expressed in terms of our ideas and what we think. And what we think is to a large extent determined by the social customs and traditions that abound in the culture that surrounds us. One school of thought says that our minds start out as blank slates upon which society tries to write the script. Social cultures exert tremendous pressure on individuals to think about things, especially things like the pursuit of happiness, along lines that are dictated by those who possess power within the society.

In the pursuit of happiness, the unrefined *motivation* (or negative temptation) of the mind is to rise in the esteem of men by exemplifying cultural ideals. If left to itself, the mind becomes preoccupied with social yardsticks that gauge success, such as the daily message of the mirror. The mind continually frets and worries about how best to measure up, and then it takes but fleeting pleasure in the gratification of vanity (if social acclaim is actually received) before sinking into a new cycle of anxiety.

But the true spiritual *role* of the mind is to seek learning, understanding, and wisdom so that it might serve as a more valuable resource to the spirit as it tries to realize its divine destiny. Gordon B. Hinckley explained that "there is incumbent upon you . . . the responsibility to observe the commandment to continue to study and to learn. Said the Lord, 'yea, seek ye out of the best books words of wisdom; seek learning, even by study and also by faith.' What a charge has been laid upon us to grow constantly toward eternity. . . . Ours must be a ceaseless quest for truth. That truth must include spiritual and religious truth as well as secular."[4] If the mind is engaged to a meaningful degree in its true spiritual role of seeking wisdom and learning, there will be precious little time for social posturing, vanity, and efforts designed to obtain the praise of men.

THE TRUE ROLE OF THE BODY, MIND, AND SPIRIT

As the students and I discuss these points, we create a chart that tries to capture the *nature*, *motivations*, and true *roles* of the body, mind, and spirit.

The True Role of the Body, Mind, and Spirit			
	Inherent Nature	Natural Motivation	True Spiritual Role
Spirit	Offspring of Deity with spiritual gifts	Express love, find meaning, develop spiritual gifts	Unite and guide body, mind, and spirit in a higher cause
Mind	Blank slate, taught to think by society	Gain esteem by living up to cultural ideals	Seek wisdom to help the spirit realize its spiritual destiny
Body	Mechanism for replicating DNA	Gratify physical sensations of pleasure	Serve as a temple for the spirit; follow the spirit

The shaded portion of the chart represents those elements of our physical and social natures that the spirit must discipline and harness if the spiritual quest is to be realized. The natural motivations (or negative temptations) of the body and mind arise from their inherent natures, and if followed without higher spiritual guidance will lead the soul away from its proper function. It is only by surrendering ourselves—body, mind, and spirit—to a higher spiritual cause that we have a hope of realizing the joy that inspired the "Impossible Dream" of Don Quixote and that animated the writings of such idealists as Thoreau, Frost, and Whitman. Unfortunately, our ongoing struggle with the mirror poses a significant threat to the successful unification of body, mind, and spirit.

ATTRACTIVENESS AT THE LEVEL OF BODY, MIND, AND SPIRIT

At this point in our discussion, it is time to reconsider the image in the mirror and to review the meaning of appearance as understood at the body, mind, and spirit levels. It is interesting to reflect that when life is lived at the *Spirit Level*, attractiveness and appearance lose their significance. In spite of its imperfections, the image in the mirror becomes a dear friend and valued partner, rather than an enemy to be scorned for not being the "fairest in the land." But for life at the body and mind levels, it is a different story.

The Body Level

At the aesthetic or body level, females are biologically tempted to cultivate sexual attractiveness as a commodity that can be exchanged on the open market for valuable resources. At best, it is swapped for protection and emotional commitment. At worst, it is bartered and casually sold for money. In either case, the male who lives his life at the aesthetic level purchases sexual attractiveness from such a female as a means of satisfying physical appetites and lust. The inner being that inhabits the sexually attractive body is of little concern, either to the owner of the body or to the person attracted by it. Following biological urges that compel one to achieve a certain level of sexual attractiveness—only to win the affection of a mate who is interested in exploiting one's attractive body for the gratification of lust—is a shallow victory indeed.

The Mind Level

At the ethical or mind level, the picture is no less bleak. Females are tempted to compete with each other to see who can be most attractive given the exclusive fashions of the day. As a sign of victory, males shower attention on those that most closely approximate the current standard of beauty. But the real intent of males who live their lives at the ethical level is to use the attractive butterfly as an ornament to enhance their own social status. When its beauty is out-lived, the butterfly is cast off with no thought for the inner soul of the being that has been discarded. Again, striving to achieve a certain level of social attractiveness—only to win the affection of a mate who is interested in using his partner's appearance to enhance his worldly standing—is a hollow triumph.

For those women and men who live life at the aesthetic and eth-ical levels, the image in the mirror will forever be a hated foe. The edict from the mirror will always be a declaration of inadequacy. Efforts to reverse the judgments of the mirror will lead to increasingly zealous measures that will only waste the energy of life without alter-ing in the least the dismal verdict.

The Spirit Level

"On the other hand, what will men and women find attractive about each other if they are fully engaged in the *Spiritual Life?*" I ask.

"For both sexes," Sarah explains after a pause, "true attractiveness will radiate from within. The eyes will express charm through the steady gaze of self-awareness and self-determination. A comeliness of form will be illuminated by actions that serve to uplift and inspire. The face will be genuine and expressive, full of concern for others. The back will be straight and firm with the resolve to live each moment of precious life to the fullest."

"People who live the *Spiritual Life*," Kristen says dreamily, "will be naturally attracted toward one another based on their common strivings for self-actualization, with physical appearance being of minor importance." Her romantic cheeks become flushed as she speaks.

"It sounds like 'twue wove,'" Matthew says solemnly. This time, even I can't keep my eyes from rolling at Matthew's wisdom.

"In contrast to relationships at the body or mind level," Carol adds, "two people who base their relationship on *spiritual* attraction will be as concerned with the inner growth and development of their companion as with the realization of their own spiritual quest. Rather than view each other as objects to be temporarily used for selfish ends, they will be concerned with creating mutual opportunities for life-long development. The attraction will grow ever stronger."

"Do such people really exist?" Brittany inquires skeptically.

All I can do in response to the last concern is smile and say, "I sincerely believe they do, and I hope that their numbers will continue to grow."

A REVIEW OF THE TRUE PATH

As a summary of the concept of eudaimonism and its three maxims, and as a contrast to the Happiness Balloon, I draw two lines that start at a single point and then grow farther apart.

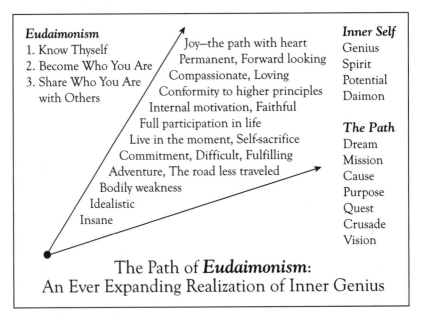

Eudaimonism
1. Know Thyself
2. Become Who You Are
3. Share Who You Are with Others

Joy—the path with heart
Permanent, Forward looking
Compassionate, Loving
Conformity to higher principles
Internal motivation, Faithful
Full participation in life
Live in the moment, Self-sacrifice
Commitment, Difficult, Fulfilling
Adventure, The road less traveled
Bodily weakness
Idealistic
Insane

Inner Self
Genius
Spirit
Potential
Daimon

The Path
Dream
Mission
Cause
Purpose
Quest
Crusade
Vision

The Path of *Eudaimonism*:
An Ever Expanding Realization of Inner Genius

On the left we list the maxims of *eudaimonism*. On the right we list two types of words—those that convey the unique nature of our inner self, and those that convey the sense of striving that we engage in as we try to understand and realize the higher purpose that our lives represent. In between the two lines that grow further apart, we list words and phrases that characterize the *eudaimonistic* process of gaining self-understanding, realizing inner potential, and contributing a verse to the "powerful play of life." We then discuss and compare these characteristics in relation to the characteristics of the Happiness Balloon.

While the things in the balloon are sought for self-gratification, the realization of the inner *daimon* is sought so that it can benefit the lives of others. As such, it represents the highest form of compassion for others (even though, paradoxically, it is initially concerned with the self in the form of self-discovery and self-development). Additionally, the joy that is realized when we strive to improve ourselves, and then see others benefit from our enhanced abilities, can never be taken away. The pleasure associated with self-gratification lasts about as long as it takes for a balloon to pop. I emphasize this last point by taking the large, yellow balloon that has been floating around the classroom and bursting it with a needle. (The force of my following statements is thereby diminished by the distraction occasioned by a piece of the balloon that, unknown to me, has landed neatly on top of my head.)

"With a *eudaimonistic* approach," I continue earnestly (oblivious to my yellow cap), "life is lived in the moment as a full participant, and joy and happiness are experienced as part of the journey, rather than being sought for at the end of the string. The balloon string," I explain, "was drawn as a straight line because it represents no inherent value or meaning, nor does it involve the realization of potential. It represents mindless drudgery. The path of *eudaimonism*, on the other hand, grows ever wider as a representation of potential that is increasingly realized over time. There is no balloon at the end, only the satisfaction of growth and sharing along the way.

"Finally," I conclude, "the path of *eudaimonism* is determined by listening to the promptings of the inner genius. The string path is dictated by biological urges, social norms, and cultural traditions. The string path is difficult because it has no meaning, involves no growth, and is inherently boring (I'm in a hurry; life's no fun; I don't know why). The *eudaimonistic* path is difficult because it requires self-sacrifice and because it represents a lifelong expenditure of energy, effort, and commitment to a higher cause. But the reward is lasting joy as opposed to the fleeting gratification of vanity or physical pleasure.

THE ROAD LESS TRAVELED CAN BE VERY BUMPY

The mood suddenly turns dark as Holly can no longer contain her dissatisfaction with my idealistic play-acting and philosophical posturing. "Are you aware," she begins with quiet wrath, "that people who are overweight in this country are discriminated against? Do you have any idea how painful it is to feel unattractive? Do you have any comprehension of what is required to let go of the belief that I will be happier if I could just lose some weight and look a little better?" Her voice becomes louder and trembles with sarcasm and emotion. "Do you think I will be happier if I stop bathing and combing my hair, and then prance around citing quips from musicals?" The tears of frustration that rim her eyes are sincere.

Having faced this line of questioning before, I am not unprepared, nor do I feel defensive—she is not the first to challenge the merit of my ideas or the worth of my teaching style. Yet I still hope that my answers can provide some guidance, if not comfort. (The shard of bright yellow balloon that I still wear like a jester's crown does not make my task any easier.) "There is a difference," I begin tentatively, "between paying attention to personal hygiene (bathing and grooming) and searching for happiness by trying to conform to arbitrary, subjective, and ever changing standards of beauty. I have not argued in favor of abandoning the former. Instead, I have sought to convince you of the futility of the latter.

"Further," I continue, "I can sympathize with the despair that arises from a ceaseless preoccupation with trying to live up to social norms. Too much of my life has been spent climbing up the string. I am also aware, from personal experience, of the types of discrimination that are leveled at obese people—job discrimination, ridicule, and unjust stereotypes to name a few. Although I cannot confess to know what it is like to feel unattractive,"—I say this jokingly as I run my fingers through the few hairs that have not yet surrendered to my receding hairline—"I do know what it is like to be discriminated against because of failure to conform."

I make this last comment as I study the piece of balloon that is now lodged between my fingers, and try to fathom how it got there. "It is also very helpful," I add, "if you don't take yourself too seriously. Perhaps the greatest way to ease our burden of despair and frustration," I instruct Holly, as I shoot my missle of elastic balloon in her direction, "is to remember that we are all just silly people who want to be attractive and appear intelligent." At last, Holly smiles through her tears. "Fortunately," I conclude, "we have better things to do.

"How would your friends and family respond," I ask, "if you were to announce that you were throwing out the bathroom scale, you were finished with diets, diet pills, and all other attempts to reduce weight or alter body size, and you would never again raise, or respond to, the issue of body size in relation to yourself or any other living being for the rest of your life?"

"They would feel sorry for you," Carol responds. "They would sit you down, take your temperature, and make an appointment for a psychiatric evaluation."

"Yes, they would think you were crazy," Holly adds. By now she has calmed down and is willing to consider the ideas that the class has been discussing. "They would worry that you were no longer think-ing clearly and that you would need someone to take care of you until you got better. Most of all, they would worry that your lack of con-cern with weight control would result in a new body size with an atomic mass that is roughly equal to Jupiter."

"They would treat you exactly the same way that Don Quixote's family and friends treated him when he announced that he was a knight," Sarah says. "Insane. And they would fear that your insanity would reflect negatively on them. They would try to talk you out of your delusion, and thereby break your spirit, or they would abandon you."

"We have normalized preoccupation with body size in our soci-ety," I explain. "An expression of sentiments to the effect that one refuses to walk to the beat of this drum is likely to be met with aston-ishment, disbelief, and denouncements of madness. Intuitively, our inner genius tells us that such a preoccupation is harmful, but it has already become deeply ingrained in us, and we are afraid to face the discrimination that following our own *eudaimonistic* path implies. The 'road less traveled' is not an easy path to take."

BEAUTY DOES NOT MATTER

"It isn't my goal," I say, "to convince anyone that they are attrac-tive. I am not going to try and get you to believe that you look 'OK,' or that you really are pretty in spite of your weight or proportions. Nor am I going to try and sell you on the notion that the choice to dis-continue an obsession with thinness and becoming attractive will be easy or that it will not have social repercussions. I do not care if you are happy with how you look," I almost shout. "What I do care about is that you appreciate the worth of your *daimon*, your ability to realize it, and the potential your life represents for good—none of which is *determined* by how you look! I want you to believe that your value is not dictated by your appearance, and then I want you to behave in a way that is consistent with such a belief!"

Brittany, the prom queen finally asks, "Does this mean that we are *never* going to talk about how to lose weight? I thought that was what this class was supposed to be about or I never would have signed up."

"That's a fair criticism," I concede. But I am angry at her question, because it means she hasn't understood what I've tried all semester to teach. I'm afraid my anger will prevent a rational response, so I refer the question back to the class. "So, what does *eudaimonism* or the *Spiritual Life* have to do with body size or physical attractiveness?"

After a pause, Sarah says very quietly, almost to herself, "Nothing."

"Thank you," I say, also very quietly. But the quietness is soon lost as my wrath spills over, my voice raises, and I am at last compelled to try and drive home the key point of this lecture one more time.

I start calmly: "To compete at the biological level, on the basis of sexual attractiveness, beauty matters. To win the rewards of conforming to social expectations and cultural traditions," I say more forcefully, "beauty matters. To realize your potential as a human being, to live life fully and passionately, and to fill the void of the heart so that it overflows with love and compassion," I conclude with all the energy of my soul, "beauty does *not* matter!"

SPIRITUAL SOLUTIONS

Due to the intercession of Jacob Marley's ghost, Ebeneezer Scrooge is given a chance to forego his preoccupation with wealth in favor of benevolence and goodwill toward others. It takes three ghosts, and many journeys, but finally the point is driven home as Scrooge is confronted with the meaningless end to which his life will come in the absence of a new direction. Once he realizes the joy that might be his by using his resources and talents to bring happiness to those around him, he expresses genuine gratitude. "I will live in the past, the present, and the future! The spirits of all three shall strive within me. Oh Jacob Marley! Heaven, and the Christmas Time be praised for this! I say it on my knees, old Jacob, on my knees."[5] The passion for the social status and power that wealth could bring was surrendered for the higher cause of uniting body, mind, and spirit in a higher purpose. As a result, "Scrooge was better than his word. He became as good a friend, as good a master, as good a man, as the good old city knew."[6]

The change of heart experienced by Scrooge (surrendering worldly pursuits in favor of spiritual intents) is reminiscent of that experienced by Alma, a priest in King Noah's court, after hearing the words of Abinidai. "Did not my father believe in the words which were delivered by the mouth of Abinidai? And according to his faith there was a mighty change wrought in his heart" (Alma 5:11–12). It is the same change of heart that was experienced by Don Quixote as he determined to mount a crusade to raise up the weak and those in need. It is the same change of heart that we must experience in order to give up our preoccupation with trying to get the mirror to tell us that we are the fairest in the land. Our life can make a difference, as President Hinckley suggests, but only if we experience a change of heart and allow the spirit to guide our destiny. "Have ye experienced this mighty change in your hearts?" (Alma 5:14).

SUMMARY

The belief that our life can make a difference is fundamental to the pursuit of happiness. But for many of us it will require a profound change of heart before we adopt this belief. In order to make a meaningful difference, our spirit is meant to unite and guide the abilities of the body and mind in accomplishing a higher purpose with our lives.

The true role of the body is to provide sensory input to the spirit, serve as a means for expressing spiritual yearnings, and to provide a holy temple in which to house the spirit. The true role of the mind is to seek learning and wisdom, both secular and spiritual, so that it might provide the spirit with the understanding necessary to fulfill its destiny.

It is the body, mind, and spirit—when united toward a common purpose—that propels the *soul* along a course of *proper function*, ultimately leading to happiness. Unfortunately, our ongoing struggle with the mirror poses a significant threat to the successful unification of body, mind, and spirit. But the struggle is futile.

Striving to achieve a certain level of sexual attractiveness—only to win the affection of admirers who are interested in exploiting one's attractive body for the gratification of lust or the enhancement of social status—is an empty conquest. In contrast, two people who base their relationship on *spiritual* attraction will be as concerned with the inner growth and development of their companion as with the realization of their own spiritual quest.

In comparison with the balloon path, the path of *eudaimonism* is oriented toward the benefit of others. It is guided by the spirit within and it leads to lasting joy. Even so, the path of *eudaimonism*, or *The Road Less Traveled*, is fraught with discrimination, lack of sympathy, and maybe even charges of lunacy. Even though it can be a bumpy road, it is the only one going in the right direction.

In order to realize spiritual potential, to live life fully and passionately, and to fill the void of the heart so that it overflows with love and compassion, beauty does not matter. What does matter is experiencing a change of heart that fosters the belief that one's life can make a difference as led by the promptings of the Spirit.

CHAPTER FIFTEEN

MAKING PEACE WITH THE IMAGE IN THE MIRROR

Nothing but an indifference to the things of this world,
and entire submission to the will of Providence here,
and a well-grounded expectation of happiness hereafter,
can give us a true satisfactory enjoyment of ourselves.
—Benjamin Franklin

Matthew kneels before Sarah at the beginning of our last class period. They are both dressed in a manner befitting the upper classes of England at the outbreak of the French Revolution (late 1700s). Matthew plays the part of Sydney Carton, while Sarah assumes the important, but nonspeaking, role of Miss Lucie Manette. They portray a sensitive scene from Dickens's classic story *A Tale of Two Cities*, in which Sydney takes the gentle hand of Lucie and expresses the following sentiment with all the passion and energy of his heart: "It is useless to say it, I know, but it rises out of my soul. For you, and for any dear to you, I would do anything. I would embrace any sacrifice. Try to hold me in your mind, at some quiet times, as ardent and sincere in this one thing. Oh, Miss Manette, . . . think now and then that there is a man who would give his life, to keep a life that you love beside you."[1]

Matthew turns in an admirable performance. Lucie, as portrayed by Sarah, is visibly touched by the declaration. "Of course, Sydney is a profligate," I explain to the class. At this clarification everyone looks at Matthew and then rolls their eyes in unison. "He spends his wasted life in the arms of pleasure," I continue. "But his one redeeming grace is his devotion to Lucie, and his devotion runs true. In the end he chooses to be executed in place of Lucie's young husband, who thereby enjoys a long and happy life 'beside' Lucie and their children. In spite of Sydney's numerous flaws, this final sacrifice dignifies him. His final words express a noble sentiment that has eluded him his entire life."

This is Matthew's cue to utter the immortal statement: "It is a far, far better thing that I do, than I have ever done; it is a far, far better rest that I go to than I have ever known." Through the subsequent applause of fellow students, both Matthew and Sydney are exonerated. Matthew returns to his seat with head held high.

"Ultimately," I explain, "it is all about the ability to care for others so deeply that we are able to rise above our own interests. The sacrifice of life, as made by Sydney, is the highest expression of genuine caring. While few of us will be required to care for others to such an extreme, the principle of selfless giving is nevertheless the same. When we observe an untainted act of pure sacrifice like Sydney's, made for the sole purpose of increasing the happiness of others, we are able see more clearly how trivial and selfish such things as fashion and wealth really are.

"For this higher level of caring to develop," I suggest with deliberate emphasis, "we must *embrace* the image in the mirror just as it is. Because it is that image—and our obedience to the spiritual light within it—that must carry the day when the chips are down and decisive action is required. It was only by reaching very deep, overcoming his haunting sense of inferiority, and acknowledging the divine light within himself that Sydney was able to act as he did. We face the same challenge if we are to do *far, far better things than we have ever done before.*"

CULTIVATE THE LIGHT WITHIN YOU

The teachings of President Gordon B. Hinckley provide *ten action steps* that if followed will allow us to make peace with the image in the mirror. "Some of you may feel," President Hinckley begins, "that you are not as attractive and beautiful and glamorous as you would like to be. Rise above any such feelings, cultivate the light you have within you, and it will shine through as a radiant expression that will be seen by others. You need never feel inferior."[2]

Once Sydney finally allowed the *light within* him to animate his deeds, that light did indeed radiate from him and even became a source of comfort to those around him. The nobility of his course and his compassion for fellow sufferers drove every feeling of inferiority from his soul.

Following President Hinckley's advice would have saved Snow White's evil stepmother a great deal of grief as well. Instead, the wicked queen allowed her feelings of inferiority to drive her to such fanatic measures that the result was her awful destruction. In addition to modern counsel from our prophet, the New Testament exerts "let not your adorning be that of plaiting the hair, and of wearing gold, or of putting on [fine] apparel; but let it be the hidden woman of the heart . . . " (2 Peter 3:25). How much happier would we be if our modern concept of "beauty" were based on virtue, modesty, cleanliness, chastity, and the expressions of the heart—or the *light within*. It is encouraging to note that such societies have existed.

For example in the Book of Mormon, when the people were most righteous, they did not wear costly apparel that distinguished the fashionable and well-to-do from the poor and ungainly. They were instead content to be *neat and comely*. Even though they were persecuted by those who derided them for their simplicity, they refused to engage in behaviors that might separate them into classes whose worth could be judged by arbitrary social yardsticks (fashion, wealth, and so on).

They esteemed all men like unto themselves on the basis of a common spiritual brotherhood. We should also strive for these attitudes and behaviors in our relations with each other (Alma 1:25–30).

As I look out over my students during our final class together, I feel that each one is exceptionally beautiful. It is not because they closely compare with the fashion models. They are beautiful because they are clean and modest. They represent the daughters of Zion, they embody virtue and nobility, and they wear the crown of faithfulness. They are beautiful to me because during the course of the semester they have each allowed me to glimpse the hidden woman of the heart. It is my prayer that they will be able to rise above a vain and pleasure-seeking society that would try to dissuade them from the truth of their preciousness. And so we come to the first of our ten steps for taking action.

1. Rise above the feelings of inadequacy that result from comparing the image in the mirror against the false and vain standards of beauty that society has established. To do this you must also follow steps two and three:

2. Refuse to engage in discussions or behavior concerning yourself or others that deal with body size, weight-loss, or any other physical trait that encourages comparison against an arbitrary standard of acceptable fashion. (This may be a challenge, but it is essential.)

3. Whenever feelings of inadequacy or inferiority arise, which they surely will, immediately recognize the source from which they come (Satan), and make every effort to cast them off before they have time to poison your heart and diminish your self-concept.

Cultivate Your Talents

"You need never feel that you were born without talents or without opportunities to give them expression," President Hinckley continues. "Cultivate whatever talents you have, and they will grow and refine and become an expression of your true self . . . "[3]

We are taught very plainly that we are children of God, and that due to our divine heritage we are each endowed with spiritual gifts, or talents, that are unique to us. "For there are many gifts, and to every man is given a gift by the Spirit of God. To some is given one, and to some is given another, that all may be profited thereby" (D&C 46:11, 12).

As indicated in this scripture, we are also clearly taught that the purpose for which we are given gifts is so that others can benefit from them. They are not given to us for our amusement, or to enhance our personal glory, or to validate our worth in comparison to others. They are given to us so that we can help and serve each other. If we neglect these gifts and talents because of an obsession with futile efforts to appease vanity, or because of a preoccupation with gratifying physical appetites, we will miss out on that which is most joyful and beneficial in this life.

Instead, the prophet counsels us to cultivate our talents so that they might become an expression of our true selves. This mindset is the key to overcoming our dissatisfaction with the image in the mirror. Rather than focus on the ways that we don't measure up, we must be willing to dedicate our lives to the discovery, development, and expression of our God-given talents.

For most of his life, Sydney of A *Tale of Two Cities* reprimanded himself for being inadequate and inferior. His escape from this self-imposed sense of unworthiness took the form of mindless pleasure-seeking as if there were no other alternative. Yet deep inside he possessed to the highest degree the spiritual gift of loving devotion. How much more good might he have done, how many more people might he have blessed, and how much greater might have been his joy had he sought out and expressed this gift earlier?

Additional action steps are offered as a framework for living so that we can take a proactive involvement in using our gifts to bless the lives of others. Much of our success will depend on what we choose to expose ourselves to. Will it be the vulgar and explicit sit-coms, soap operas, films, and books that promote selfish pleasure-seeking and social vanity? Or will we expose ourselves to those things which are *virtuous, lovely, of good report,* and *praiseworthy.*

4. You must believe that you are endowed from above with wonderful spiritual gifts. Pray, ponder, meditate, and seek spiritual guidance often as to the nature of your unique gifts.

5. Make *specific* plans to expose yourself to new ideas through scripture study; attendance at various religious or secular instructional courses; study from the best books of men; attentive listening to conference, sacrament meeting, and public speakers; and deep philo-sophical inquiry through discussions with family members, friends, teachers, and leaders.

6. Step out of the daily rut to engage in new, carefully planned experiences that will be a source of insight. This may be in the form of travel, new avenues of volunteer or professional work, new creative efforts (art, music, poetry, literature, and so on), or any number of experiences that will be beneficial to self-understanding and that have previously been neglected due to time, energy, fear, or preoccupation with the mirror.

7. As insights are developed in relation to talents and spiritual gifts, seek new ways to express these gifts on behalf of others. Infuse all the roles of your life—parent, sibling, child, colleague, church worker, spouse, volunteer—with all of the vitality and insight that these newly opened gifts provide. Continually strive to expand the number of those impacted by your talents until you have blessed the entire world, if possible. Remember, "thou hast been faithful over a few things, I will make thee a ruler over many things . . . " (Matthew 25:21).

TRY A LITTLE HARDER

"In summary," President Hinckley says, "try a little harder to measure up to the divine within each of you. As Alma said, 'Awake and arouse your faculties.'"[4]

It is so easy to allow our lives to become full of the trivia and drudgery that robs us of precious energy. There is an old saying that "You must become who you are, or you will become what you do." In other words, if we do not become who we are by seeking out, developing, and expressing the spiritual gifts that we have, then our life will represent little more than the mundane trivia with which it is filled.

It was not until he remembered his promise to Lucie, and not until her husband's life was threatened with execution, that Sydney finally rose to the occasion and made a personal sacrifice for the happiness of another. Don Quixote, on the other hand, took a more proactive approach by reading books from morning until night and pondering how he might make the world a better place. He at last formulated a specific plan, to become a knight errant, and then deliberately put his plan into effect. While some derided him for pursuing his difficult quest, he brought dignity to his own life and inspiration to the lives of others as he sought to use the strength of his good right arm to raise up the weak and those in need.

By relying on chance circumstance to supply an opportunity for action, Sydney may have missed the occasion to follow the light within. It is the approach of Sir Quixote that is more likely to guarantee that we can become who we truly are. But to accomplish that, we must heed the encouragement of the prophet Gordon B. Hinckley to "try harder." Just as it took Don Quixote great pains in terms of study, meditation, and preparation before he was able to take up the lance and shield, we must also pay a price of diligent study and spiritual preparation as suggested in the final action steps listed here.

8. We must be proactive in our determination to measure up to the divine within us; we cannot rely on chance circumstance to inspire greatness. The greatness is already there, and while the day lasts there is a pressing need to put forth the effort necessary to develop and express that greatness for the benefit of others. And it is the genuine love for others that must be the inspiration for this work.

9. Do not worry so much about winning love from others, *instead worry about expressing love to them.* President Hinckley declares that "[love] is a beacon of hope in a world of distress."[5] In the scriptures we are taught to "*love* one another," not to "*seek* love from one another" or to "*be in* love with one another." *Love* is the active verb that requires us to appreciate the divine worth of all God's children and to accept our responsibility to serve and bless them. This is the type of love that the Savior has asked us to develop.

WHAT ABOUT OTHERS?

"You know," Carol sighs, "this has been a good class for me personally. I have learned a lot about myself, and I have some specific ideas of where to go from here. But what about my husband? I want to move on to the *Spiritual Life*, but he is still firmly entrenched in the *Aesthetic* and *Ethical Life*. Sometimes I feel my usefulness to him is more for the gratification of his lust and the enhancement of his social status, than it is to be a soul mate on a great spiritual quest. He regularly expresses concern about how much I weigh, for example, or what I look like. It drives me crazy and makes me feel horrible about myself. How do I rise to the spiritual level, when he isn't interested in working toward it with me? When I try to talk to him about the things we have been learning in this class, he has no interest. In fact, it irritates him."

This particular concern has been expressed every time I teach this course, and I still haven't found a satisfactory answer. In general it seems that women are more concerned than men with the emotional and spiritual aspects of human existence. Men are more likely to be content if they are well fed, have regular intimacy, and are in possession of the remote control. While women share some of the same basic needs as men, they tend to have a greater sense of longing for a higher spiritual quest, a quest that is enthusiastically shared and supported by a companion who is also a soul mate. What should they do if their companion not only does not share that vision, but in fact represents a millstone that suppresses it? For many women it is a discouraging dilemma.

"Carol," I begin tentatively, "you highlight a difficult situation. All of us in this room are directly influenced, and maybe even hampered, by the lack of spiritual inspiration among some of those that we love most dearly. Our natural tendency is to want to force our insights into their minds, and then bind them to live up to what they know. It is frustrating when it seems that their minds are closed to our influence. As such, I believe that our most prudent course is to grant them their free agency, while fully exercising ours.

"By *fully exercising ours*," I continue, "I mean that while allowing them to chart their own course in life, we must turn our gaze inward and seek divine inspiration in charting our own course. I believe with all my heart that if we will set a true course and focus our attention on steering our own ship that in many cases those that we love will of their own accord follow in our wake. As Henry David Thoreau expressed, 'Though we may not arrive at our port within a calculable period, we would preserve the true course.' As we preserve the true course, we will become a beacon for others to follow. We will obtain the best results as we lead out in inner growth and development, rather than attempting to push from the rear. But in the end, there is no guarantee that others will do as we desire or that our lives will be free from disappointment. Life is hard." Based on Carol's concern, a final action step is in order:

10. Focus first on changing yourself, not others. Recognize that all people have their free agency and that the spiritual progress of some will be slow (or nonexistent) for self-imposed reasons. At the same time, you are still free to make a personal commitment in relation to your own development. It is true that the actions and attitudes of others can definitely impact the quality of life and the amount of resources available to devote to one's spiritual quest. But it is also true that no one can prevent the spiritual development of someone who is inspired and determined to grow.

Finally, it is important to understand that the spiritual growth of one individual can have only a positive influence on the spiritual development of those who are closest to him or her. The best way to change others is not through direct persuasion or coercion, but through the inspiration that emanates from our own spiritual development.

LAY DOWN THE BURDEN; BE LIFTED IN JOY

When we believe that our adequacy and worth is measured directly by the appearance of our image, we carry a great burden. The burden is characterized by anxiety, self-deprecation, and futile strivings to change the mostly unchangeable nature of our physical appearance. There is a great sense of relief when one is finally able to accept the image in the mirror unconditionally with all of its imperfections and inadequacies (and with all of its newfound talents).

Rather than fret about whether or not the image is perfect enough to satisfy the demands of vanity, the focus of attention is on appreciating the value of the inner being that peers through the image. It is also on building up the health and physical capacity of the outer image so that it might properly house the spirit and carry out its spiritual directives. We graciously accept the image in the mirror as a reflection of the physical element of a united soul. We accept the image and assume the responsibility to behave in a way that will honor the sacred role that it plays in furthering the progress of our spiritual destiny. By doing these things we lay down a tremendous burden that we will never have to carry again.

Not only will we lay down a wearisome burden, but as we place our trust in the prophet's counsel by striving to rise above our feelings of inferiority, seeking to cultivate the spiritual talents which are surely ours, and finding expression for those talents in ways that benefit others, the result will be joy. Rather than with wealth, or with pearls, or with fine robes, the Lord has said that he "will crown the faithful with joy and rejoicing" (D&C 52:43). In this promise, we find the true path to happiness.

SPIRITUAL SOLUTIONS

Unable to end our final class together without one more attempt at playacting, I hold up ancient pictures of former students at BYU. With the voice of Jonathan Keating from *Dead Poet's Society*, I hauntingly say to the class, "They're not that much different from you, are they? Same haircuts, invincible—just like you feel. The world is their oyster. They believe they are destined for great things, just like many of you. Their eyes are full of hope, just like yours. Did they wait until it was too late to make of their lives even one iota of what they were capable? These students are now fertilizing daffodils. Lean in if you want to hear their legacy to you. *Carpe. Carpe Diem*. Seize the day, girls (and Matthew). Make your lives extraordinary."

"Sydney Carton," I explain, "waited almost until it was too late to make his life extraordinary. Without the unusual circumstances of the French revolution, he may never have engaged in a single act worthy of his inner greatness. He may have altogether missed the joy that can only be experienced by offering a gift of yourself on behalf of another—a gift only you can give. We must not neglect the opportunity that this life affords to refine our spiritual nature and to then extend to those within our reach the blessings that arise from our unique spiritual gifts.

Yet Sydney did find a way to give that gift. It is in the example of men like him that we see literally exemplified the scripture which says, "For whosoever will save his life shall lose it. But whosoever shall lose his life for my name's sake shall save it" (Mark 8:35, 36). When Sydney *lost* his life out of devotion to Lucie, his life *found* a dignity and meaning that it had never known—and may never have known otherwise. Likewise, our true life—the one that is dignified and ennobled with selfless acts of divine service—will never be *found* unless we *lose* our other life—the one that is characterized by the blind pursuit of physical pleasure and social praise. When we follow this course based on our commitment to the name of Christ, then we not only find a noble and dignified life on earth, but we increase our hope for eternal life. In the end, it is our love for Christ that serves as the true polar star from which we might chart a sure course.

Brittany's Promise

As the final bell rings, the look on Brittany's face expresses extreme disappointment and dissatisfaction at not having learned anything about weight control. "If we need our body to be healthy and be a temple for our spirit, then why can't we learn about weight control," she asks out loud, "or at least learn what a healthy weight is and how to achieve it?"

"That," I suggest, "will be a good place to start next semester."

"That's nice," she says, "but I won't be here unless you promise right now that we'll actually talk about weight control."

"I promise," I say. "But we will only talk about it from a health perspective, and then only if *you* promise that the *only* reason that you will attend is to learn how to be healthier—not how to lose weight so that you can look better."

Brittany sighs deeply and then says, "Okay, I promise."

Farewell

As each semester ends and students go their way, it is time to bid farewell to friends that I have grown close to but in all probability will never see again. I am always sorry to see them go, but glad for the opportunity I've had to tread a common path with them for a short time.

As we come to the close of the semester and to the close of this book, I hope that I, my students, and all those readers who have endured this far will be a step closer to understanding the principle taught by Sydney Carton's life. I also hope we will be a step closer to heeding the words that President Gordon B. Hinckley has spoken that apply so well to making peace with the image in the mirror:

"Some of you may feel that you are not as attractive and beautiful and glamorous as you would like to be. Rise above any such feelings, cultivate the light you have within you, and it will shine through as a radiant expression that will be seen by others. You need never feel inferior. You need never feel that you were born without talents or without opportunities to give them expression. Cultivate whatever talents you have, and they will grow and refine and become an expression of your true self appreciated by others. In summary, try a little harder to measure up to the divine within each of you."[5]

TEN STEPS FOR TAKING ACTION

In parting, I encourage all of us to remember the ten steps for taking action:

1. Rise above the feelings of inadequacy that result from comparing the image in the mirror against the false and vain standards of beauty that society has established.

2. Refuse to engage in discussions or behaviors concerning yourself or others that deal with body size, weight-loss, or any other physical trait that encourages comparison.

3. When feelings of inadequacy or inferiority arise, make every effort to cast them off before they have time to poison your heart and diminish your sense of self-worth.

4. Believe that you are endowed from above with wonderful

spiritual gifts. Pray, ponder, meditate, and seek spiritual guidance often as to the nature of your unique gifts.

5. Make *specific* plans to expose yourself to new ideas through study, reading, and listening to others.

6. Step out of the daily rut to engage in new, carefully planned experiences that will be a source of insight.

7. As insights are developed in relation to talents and spiritual gifts, seek new ways to express these gifts on behalf of others. Continually strive to expand the number of those impacted by your talents until you have blessed the entire world within your reach.

8. Be proactive in the determination to measure up to the divine within. The greatness is already there, and while the day lasts there is a pressing need to put forth the effort necessary to develop and express that greatness for the benefit of others.

9. Do not worry so much about winning love from others, instead worry about expressing love to them. *Love* is an active verb that requires us to appreciate the divine worth of all God's children and to accept our responsibility to serve and bless them.

10. Focus on changing yourself, not others. Often, the best way to change others is not through direct persuasion or coercion, but through the inspiration that emanates from our own spiritual development.

ENDNOTES

INTRODUCTION

1. "Snow White," in *The Complete Fairy Tales of the Brothers Grimm*, ed. Jack Zipes (New York: Bantam Books, 1987), 196–204.
2. Ann Oldenburg, "Boomers Believe They've Found a Fountain of Youth in a Syringe," *USA Today*, 15 November 2000, 1A, 16A, 10D.
3. Karen S. Schneider, "Mission Impossible," *People Weekly*, 3 June 1996, 67.

CHAPTER ONE

Opening quotation: Benjamin Franklin, *Poor Richard's Almanac* (New York: John B. Alden, 1889).

1. "1997 Body Image Survey Findings," *Psychology Today* (January/February 1997):32–44, 75–76, 78, 84.
2. Jean Kilbourne, *Slim Hopes: Advertising and the Obsession with Thinness* (Northampton, MA: Media Education Foundation, 1995), video. Also Karen S. Schneider, "Mission Impossible," *People Weekly*, 3 June 1996, 71.
3. As quoted by Karen S. Schneider, "Mission Impossible," *People Weekly*, 3 June 1996, 66. See also Mary Pipher, *Reviving Ophelia* (New York: G.P. Putnam's Sons, 1994).

CHAPTER TWO

Opening quotation: Joseph Smith, *The Words of Joseph Smith*, edited by Andrew F. Ehat and Lyndon W. Cook (Provo, UT: Brigham Young University Religious Studies Center, 1980), 348.

1. Karen S. Schneider, "Mission Impossible," *People Weekly*, 3 June 1996, 71.
2. S. Rubenstein, and B. Caballero, "Is Miss America an undernourished role model?" *Journal of the American Medical Association* 283(22–29 Mar 2000): 1569.
3. Karen S. Schneider, "Mission Impossible," *People Weekly*, 3 June 1996, 65.
4. S. L. Gortmaker, A. Must, J. M. Perrin, A. M. Sobol, and W. H. Dietz, "Social and Economic Consequences of Overweight in Adolescence and Young Adulthood," *New England Journal of Medicine* 329(14):1008–12 (1983).
5. Gary Larson, *The Prehistory of the Far Side: A 10th Anniversary Exhibit* (New York: Andrews and McMeel, 1989), 250.
6. "1997 Body Image Survey Findings," *Psychology Today* (January/February 1997):32–44, 75–76, 78, 84.
7. James Dobson, *What Wives Wish Their Husbands Knew About Women* (Wheaton, Illinois: Tyndale House Publishers, 1975), 59.

8. "1997 Body Image Survey Findings," *Psychology Today* (January/February 1997):32–44, 75–76, 78, 84.
9. Rita Rubin, "Health Guide: Fat and Fit," *U.S. News & World Report,* 16 May 1994, 67.

CHAPTER THREE

Opening quotation: Benjamin Franklin, *On True Happiness* (New York: n.p., 1958).
1. Theodore Dreiser, *Sister Carrie* (New York: Bantam Classic, 1982), 398.
2. Ibid., back cover.
3. Abraham H. Maslow, *Toward a Psychology of Being,* 2d ed. (New York: Van Nostrand Reinhold, 1968).

CHAPTER FOUR

Opening quotation: François, Duc de La Rochefoucauld, *Reflections or Sentences and Moral Maxims* (New York: J. Pott, 1904), 23.
1. "Losing It in Public," *Newsweek,* 10 February 1997, 54.

CHAPTER FIVE

Opening quotation: Francis Bacon, "Of Wisdom for a Man's Self," *Essays* (Amherst, N.Y.: Prometheus Books, 1995).
1. James Dobson, *What Wives Wish Their Husbands Knew About Women* (Wheaton, Illinois: Tyndale House Publishers, 1975), 41.
2. As quoted at the following web site: http://home2.planetinternet.be/ver-jans/Singing_Divas/Quotes/
3. David G. Myers, *The Pursuit of Happiness: Discovering the Pathway to Fulfillment, Well-Being, and Enduring Personal Joy* (New York: Avon Books, 1993).

CHAPTER SIX

Opening quotation: David O. McKay, *Gospel Ideals* (Salt Lake City: Improvement Era, 1953), 129.
1. Gordon B. Hinckley, "I Believe," *Ensign,* August 1992, 6.

CHAPTER SEVEN

1. Henry David Thoreau, *Walden and Other Writings* (New York: Bantam Books, 1982), 172–3.
2. Sharon Begley, "You're OK, I'm Terrific: 'Self-Esteem' Backfires," *Newsweek,* 13 July 1998, 69.
3. Ibid. See also "Narcissism, Self-Esteem, and Aggression," *Harvard Mental Health Letter* 15(12):7 (June 1999). See also B. J. Bushman and R. F. Baumeister, "Threatened Egotism, Narcissism, Self-Esteem, and Direct

Displaced Aggression: Does Self-Love or Self-Hate Lead to Violence?" *Journal of Personality and Social Psychology* 75(1):219–29 (July 1998).

4. See Mary Pipher, *Reviving Ophelia* (New York: G.P. Putnam's Sons, 1994).

CHAPTER EIGHT

Opening quotation: Johann Wolfgang von Goethe, *Faust* (Chicago: Encyclopedia Britannica, 1982).

1. Henry David Thoreau, *Walden and Other Writings* (New York: Bantam Books, 1982), 172.

2. Jennifer Lee Carrell, "Newton's Vice," *Smithsonian* 31(9):130–44 (December 2000).

3. Carol Dweck, as reported in "Praise," *Hope Healthletter* 17(10):5 (October 1997).

4. C. Davis, G. Claridge, and J. Fox, "Not Just a Pretty Face: Physical Attractiveness and Perfectionism in the Risk for Eating Disorders," *International Journal of Eating Disorders*, 27(2000):67–73.

CHAPTER NINE

Opening quotation: Neal A. Maxwell, *The Smallest Part* (Salt Lake City: Deseret Book Company, 1973), 59.

CHAPTER TEN

Opening quotation: Benjamin Franklin, *On True Happiness* (New York: n.p., 1958).

1. For a brief overview of Aristotle's philosophy about *eudaimonia* (happiness), see G. B. Kerferd, "Aristotle: Ethics and Politics," in *The Encyclopedia of Philosophy*, ed. Paul Edwards, 8 vols. (New York: Macmillan Publishing, 1967), 1:161–62.

2. See Søren Kierkegaard, *Either/Or*, trans. David F. Swenson and Lillian Marvin Swenson with revision and foreword by Howard A. Johnson (Garden City: Doubleday Anchor Books, 1959). See also Søren Kierkegaard, *Fear and Trembling and The Sickness Unto Death*, trans. Walter Lowrie (Garden City: Doubleday Anchor Books, n.d.). See also David Norton, *Personal Destinies: A Philosophy of Ethical Individualism* (Princeton, NJ: Princeton University Press, 1976). Of particular interest is chapter three which deals with Kierkegaard's stages of life (aesthetic, ethical, and spiritual) as they relate to *eudaimonism*. See also Bruce H. Kirmmse, *Kierkegaard in Golden Age Denmark* (Bloomington, IN: Indiana University Press, 1990). See also Alasdair MacIntyre, "Kierkegaard, Soren Aabye," in *The Encyclopedia of Philosophy*, ed. Paul Edwards, 8 vols. (New York: Macmillan Publishing, 1967), 4:336–40.

3. Janette S. Carter, Jacqueline A. Pugh, and Ana Monterrosa, "Non-Insulin

Dependent Diabetes Mellitus in Minorities in the United States," *Annals of Internal Medicine* 125 (1 August 1996):221–32.

4. For an interesting discussion of the theory that DNA replication and genetic programming guides human behavior see Richard Dawkins, *The Selfish Gene* (New York: Oxford University Press, 1989).

5. Charles Bishop, "Cultural and biological adaptations to deprivation: the Northern Ojibwa case," in *Extinction and Survival in Human Populations*, Charles Laughlin and Ivan Brady, eds. (New York: Columbia University Press, 1978), 208–30. See also Ancel Keys et al., *The Biology of Human Starvation*, 2 vols. (Minneapolis: University of Minnesota Press, 1950).

6. Barbara Millen Posner et al., "Secular Trends in Diet and Risk Factors for Cardiovascular Disease: The Framingham Study," *Journal of the American Dietetics Association* 95 (2):171–79 (February 1995).

7. "A Report of the Surgeon General: Physical Activity and Health," *Centers for Disease Control* (11 July 1996). See also National Wellness Association, "Landmark Report Extols Benefits of Moderate Exercise," *Health Issues Update* 4(2):1–2 (Summer 1996).

8. A. H. Mokdad, et al., "The spread of the obesity epidemic in the United States, 1991–1998," *The Journal of the American Medical Association* 282 (1999):1519–22. Also A. H. Mokdad, et al., "The continuing epidemic of obesity in the United States," *The Journal of the American Medical Association* 284 (2000):1650–51.

9. Anthony Walsh, "The Biological Relationship between Sex and Love," *Free Inquiry* 11(3):20–24 (Summer 1991).

10. Ibid.

11. F. Rodriguez de Fonseca and M. Navarro, "Role of the Limbic System in Dependence on Drugs," *Annals of Medicine* 30(4):397–405 (August 1998).

12. F. S. Coleman and J. Kay, "Biology of Addiction," *Obstetric and Gynecological Clinician in North America* 25(1):1–19 (March 1998).

CHAPTER ELEVEN

Opening quotation: Benjamin Franklin, letter to Madame Brillon.

1. See chapter two, "Wealth and Well-Being," in David G. Myers, *The Pursuit of Happiness: Discovering the Pathway to Fulfillment, Well-Being, and Enduring Personal Joy* (New York: Avon Books, 1993), 31–46.

CHAPTER TWELVE

Opening quotation: Joseph Smith, *History of The Church of Jesus Christ of Latter-day Saints*, 7 vols., B. H. Roberts, ed. (Salt Lake City: The Church of Jesus Christ of Latter-day Saints, 1932–1951) 6:240.

1. Viktor Frankl, *Man's Search for Meaning* (New York: Washington Square Press, 1984), introduction.

2. Geoffrey Cowley, "The Biology of Beauty," *Newsweek*, 3 June 1996, 60.

3. See Claudia Kalb, "Our Quest to Be Perfect," *Newsweek*, 9 August 1999, 52–59. See also Doug Podolsky, "The Price of Vanity," *U.S. News & World Report*, 14 October 1996, 72–79.
4. Ann Oldenburg, "Boomers Believe They've Found a Fountain of Youth in a Syringe," *USA Today*, 15 November 2000, 1A, 16A, 10D.
5. Karen S. Schneider, "Mission Impossible," *People Weekly*, 3 June 1996, 71.
6. "1997 Body Image Survey Findings," *Psychology Today* (January/February 1997):32–44, 75–76, 78, 84.
7. Carla Treloar, Jennifer Porteous, Fatma Hassan, et al., "The Cross Cultural Context of Obesity: An INCLEN Multicentre Collaborative Study," *Health & Place* 5 (1999):279–86.
8. Rita Rubin, "Health Guide: Fat and Fit," *U.S. News & World Report*, 16 May 1994, 67.
9. G. A. Britton, "A Review of Women and Tobacco: Have We Come Such a Long Way?" *Journal of Obstetric and Gynecological Neonatal Nursing* 27(3):241–9 (May–June 1998).
10. Lynn Quenan and Patrick L. Remington, "Progress in Cancer Control in Wisconsin," *Wisconsin Medical Journal* 99(3):34–8 (June 2000).
11. "1997 Body Image Survey Findings," *Psychology Today* (January/February 1997):32–44, 75–76, 78, 84.

CHAPTER THIRTEEN

Opening quotation: Joseph Smith, *History of The Church of Jesus Christ of Latter-day Saints*, 7 vols., B. H. Roberts, ed. (Salt Lake City: The Church of Jesus Christ of Latter-day Saints, 1932–1951) 4:227.
1. For a complete discussion of how *eudaimonism* applies to modern life, see David Norton, *Personal Destinies: A Philosophy of Ethical Individualism* (Princeton, NJ: Princeton University Press, 1976). Of particular interest is chapter three which deals with Kierkegaard's stages of life (aesthetic, ethical, and spiritual) as they relate to *eudaimonism*.
2. See chapter two, "Wealth and Well-Being," in David G. Myers, *The Pursuit of Happiness: Discovering the Pathway to Fulfillment, Well-Being, and Enduring Personal Joy* (New York: Avon Books, 1993), 31–46.
3. Henry David Thoreau, *Walden and Other Writings* (New York: Bantam Books, 1982), 265.
4. Ibid.
5. Gordon B. Hinckley, "The Light Within You," *Ensign*, May 1995.
6. Ibid.
7. Ibid.

CHAPTER FOURTEEN

Opening quotation: Gordon B. Hinckley, *Teachings of Gordon B. Hinckley* (Salt Lake City: Deseret Book, 1997), 159.

1. Charles Dickens, *A Christmas Carol* (New York: Oxford University Press, 1976), 21–22.
2. Gordon B. Hinckley, "God Hath Not Given Us the Spirit of Fear," *Ensign*, October 1984, 2.
3. Joseph Smith, *History of The Church of Jesus Christ of Latter-day Saints*, 7 vols., B. H. Roberts, ed. (Salt Lake City: The Church of Jesus Christ of Latter-day Saints, 1932–1951), 4:227.
4. Gordon B. Hinckley, "The Light Within You," *Ensign*, May 1995.
5. Charles Dickens, *A Christmas Carol* (New York: Oxford University Press, 1976), 91.
6. Ibid., 98.

CHAPTER FIFTEEN

Opening quotation: Benjamin Franklin, *On True Happiness* (New York: n.p., 1958).
1. Charles Dickens, *A Tale of Two Cities* (New York: Nelson Doubleday, n.d.), 146.
2. Gordon B. Hinckley, "The Light Within You," *Ensign*, May 1995, 99.
3. Ibid.
4. Ibid.
5. Ibid.

INDEX

self, preoccupation with, 59–60
self-acceptance, 27, 29–30, 87,
199; weight and, 7
self-actualization, 21, 27, 184
self-assessment, 49, 96; unhealthy,
98
self-discipline, 184
self-discovery, 99, 173, 175
self-esteem: misguided search for,
10; not improved by weight
loss, 11; low, 18; definitions of,
80–81; true path to, 97–98
self-expression, 33, 170
self-hatred, 44, 189; due to obesity,
192
self-importance, 52, 83
self-improvement, 191, 204
self-indulgence, 132
self-respect, 79
self-sacrifice, 62, 192, 204
self-worth, 46; and love, 42; false
enhancement of, 85–86;
eternal, 94–95; measurement
of, 96; constant value of, 111;
as gift from God, 112
selfishness, 58–59, 79
selfless thinking, 69, 79
selflessness, 59, 99, 199, 209
sensuality, 125
servants, unprofitable, 113
service, 60, 79, 203; and happiness,
69, 115; education as
preparation for, 94; developing
capacity for, 116
simplicity, 79–80
Sister Carrie, 26
size discrimination, 16
Smith, Joseph: on choosing the
right, 15; on unrighteous
competition, 154; on love of
God, 167
Snow White, story of, vii-x

social expectations, 150
social indifference, 61
social norms: conformity to, 88;
and thought patterns, 138;
regarding obesity, 147
social problems, self-esteem and,
80
society: trends in, 132; pressures of,
139, 186; faults of, 140
souls, worth of, 111
spiritual guidance, 163
spiritual influence, 115–16
spiritual life, 122, 169
spiritual potential, 13
spirituality, 73, 189, 206;
components of, 170
spouse: concern for, 72; selection
of, 161–62, 189
studies: on size discrimination, 16;
on friendliness, 60–61; on
weight and beauty, 159
success, 56; material, 26; false
indicators of, 83
superiority, 58
surveys: on attitudes toward body
size, 7, 17; on personal
appearance, 11–12; on
attitudes toward thinness,
19–21; on physical attraction,
161; on body image, 162
survival, fight for, 125
tactfulness vs. honesty, 53
Tale of Two Cities, A, 198–99
talents: basing self-esteem on, 56,
100; purpose of, 61–62;
diversity of, 85; development
of, 100, 116, 175; sharing,
102–3, 177–78; parable of,
105; accountability for, 106–9,
202
teaching, 179–80

ABOUT THE AUTHOR

Steven R. Hawks is an associate professor of health science at Brigham Young University. He received a B.A. in East Asian Studies, an M.A. in International and Area Studies, an M.B.A. in Business Administration, and an Ed.D. in Health Education. He has lectured for many years at BYU Education Week on body image and self-acceptance.

Brother Hawks and his wife, Jaylyn, have five children. They reside in Payson, Utah.